Wrapped in Comfort

Knitted Lace Shawls

ALISON JEPPSON HYDE

Martingale®
& COMPANY

Wrapped in Comfort: Knitted Lace Shawls
© 2007 by Alison Jeppson Hyde

Martingale & Company
20205 144th Ave. NE
Woodinville, WA 98072-8478 USA
www.martingale-pub.com

Printed in China
12 11 10 09 08 07   8 7 6 5 4 3 2 1

Library of Congress Cataloging-in-Publication Data
Library of Congress Control Number: 2007006744

ISBN: 978-1-56477-751-5

Credits
President & CEO: Tom Wierzbicki
Publisher: Jane Hamada
Editorial Director: Mary V. Green
Managing Editor: Tina Cook
Technical Editor: Donna Druchunas
Copy Editor: Liz McGehee
Design Director: Stan Green
Illustrator: Robin Strobel
Cover & Text Designer: Stan Green
Photographer: Brent Kane

Mission Statement
Dedicated to providing quality products
and service to inspire creativity.

Contents

My Story

I ONCE SENT OFF to a sheep station in Australia for their wool rovings. A package arrived with a handwritten letter from the owner, reminiscing over a vacation that had included my town in California. She described my favorite restaurant and wondered if I, too, had ever eaten there.

Oh yes. When my husband and I moved here in '87, his company put us up in a hotel for a month while we waited to close on our house. They paid for us to eat out, a mixed blessing when you have three children under five years old to keep cheerful and well behaved night after night at their hungriest and most impatient. We quickly learned where to go and that Sue was the waitress to ask for. We adored her, and she us.

Michelle, our third child, took her first steps during our days on that corporate account. With paying for a California house, and a fourth child a year later, our visits to Sue's restaurant, or any other for that matter, became quite rare. And then one night, much later, there we were and we lucked out— we got Sue again! She was still there!

How many waitresses can reminisce, a dozen years after the fact, over what your small child had liked to order way back when? Lobster and fresh-squeezed orange juice every time, several times a week, for our oldest. Where we'd moved from, in the right season, you could buy a lobster for $1.79, and that's what Jennie had wanted again: a link between her new home and her old. The corporation didn't care in the least what a preschooler had for dinner as long as it was within their standard budget. It was.

And then Jennie was off to college. And I ran into Sue again at my medical clinic. "You're here? Hi!" The unasked question was, "Why?" We both so much wanted to tell each other how much life had changed, but neither of us quite knew whether we could to someone we, truth be told, really didn't know well at all. We were always so glad to see each other, but did that give us permission to really open up when our lives were upended? In the end, neither of us said much just then. But Sue surprised me by dropping everything to walk me down the long hallway to the elevator and then actually going up the elevator with me toward my appointment. Reluctant to let the connection go, we found ourselves talking about the kids. My, how they grow. A safe subject. Then finally she went back downstairs and I to my own doctor.

The departments on the floor where I'd found Sue were X-ray and oncology. And so it was that one of our kids told Sue over a dinner at the restaurant, a number of months later, that I had lupus. I was glad Michelle didn't pile on the details; she just took a few baby steps into the subject. Lupus, plus the cane that I'd walked in with this time, conveyed enough. I asked Sue if she minded my asking about her physical change. A tumor. They'd gotten the news since the day I'd seen her downstairs.

We'd both known. And now we knew a little more. We were so glad to see each other again, back in our normal spots. (I would gladly have sprung out of my chair in an instant and been the one serving her.) Living apparently normally in spite of the unsaid. Understanding.

A few years later, my husband took me out to dinner to spring an idea on me. He wanted a favorable reaction, so he took me to one of my favorite places. I had no idea it was coming. I was pretty distracted. I wanted Sue, was she around that night? No. "Rats," I said, "I hope she's OK." Our waitress told us that yes, Sue still worked there; we'd just come on the wrong night to catch her. Meantime, I had something I'd wanted to mention to my husband and told him that now that our Michelle was off at college, I needed help getting some more of my patterns up on my Web site. It bugged me that I couldn't remember how to do it myself. He's the Silicon Valley dweeb, would he have any time to work on it in the next little bit?

"No," he responded, surprising me. It was the perfect opening he'd been looking for. "You need to write a knitting book. You won't be happy till you do. You've had one in you for a long time. Do it." And so this book came to be written. And having long wanted to knit something for Sue, I now had an excuse. But I still owe a note back to that woman in Australia.

Helpful Hints for Lace Knitting

*M*Y MOTHER, who is 76 and has been knitting since college, offered to knit my sister Marian a scarf out of any stitch pattern she liked. Marian chose Barbara Walker's Shower Stitch, and Mom thought, "OK," and tried. And tried, until she finally put down her needles and declared she was not a lace knitter.

I use that Shower Stitch, knit from the top down for a completely different effect, to make the jellyfish in my Monterey Shawl on page 43, the most difficult pattern in this book. I taught myself how to knit lace from Barbara Walker's stitch treasuries, starting and stumbling around with patterns she specifically noted as being easy for beginners rather than trying to start with one of the hardest. Step by step and row by row, I worked toward getting a feel for how decreases and increases and yarn overs work together—and how to take them apart when need be.

I reminded Mom of the lace baby booties and sweaters she'd made for my siblings and me ages earlier. "Start again easy," I encouraged, "work your way up. It's not hard."

Today, I offer the same advice to you. The following sections include some tips I've learned along the way.

Skill Levels

If you're new to lace knitting, the scarf patterns on pages 21, 56, and 76 are great projects for practicing lace patterns with a smaller number of stitches. The Julia's Shawl pattern on page 38 was designed specifically to be as simple as possible, with an easy six-stitch repeat throughout, plus it is a great canvas for showing off a hand-painted yarn. If you're an adventurous or experienced lace knitter, you'll find shawls that range from that easy project on up to the advanced Wanda's Flowers Shawl on page 29, with a variety of patterns in between.

Knitting Needles

To make a circular shawl working back and forth, it's best that you work on a circular needle long enough to hold at least 200 stitches. My needles are 32" to 40" long. For knitting a scarf, you can use straight or circular needles, whichever you prefer.

■□□□ Beginner: Projects for first-time lace knitters using very easy stitches.

■■□□ Easy: Projects using basic stitches and repetitive stitch patterns that are mindless enough that you should not need to look at the lace pattern past the first glance if you have any experience knitting lace.

■■■□ Intermediate: Projects using a variety of lace stitches and fine yarns that are difficult to handle.

■■■■ Experienced: Projects using advanced lace-knitting techniques and stitches, including patterns that have yarn overs and decreases on both right-side and wrong-side rows.

Yarn

I used yarns of many different weights for the shawls and scarves in this book. In most cases, I used a needle size larger than what is normally recommended, to create a loose and fluid lace fabric.

Some yarn is available both in skeins and on cones. Often the coned yarn is less expensive than the skeined yarn. If you buy yarn on cones, you can knit directly from the cone or you can make your own skeins and scour (wash in hot water) the yarn to remove the spinning oil before knitting with it. I prefer working with scoured yarn.

Recently a knitter asked me about knitting from cones and where to break it off into individual balls when winding it off the cone. I said, "Why break it? Make one big hank, scour that, and wind it into a giant ball. There are no yarn ends to work in anywhere. What's not to like?" And she responded, "Oh!"

Gauge

Measuring gauge in lace patterns is a little different from measuring gauge over plain knitting. Because the yarn overs make holes in the knitting, and the stitches in every row are different, it is impossible to measure the number of stitches per inch and get a consistent result. Instead, I knit an entire repeat of the lace pattern I will be using and measure the width of that piece to determine gauge.

I only provide stitch gauge for my lace patterns. Row gauge is not critical because you can simply knit a scarf or shawl to the desired length. The gauge for lace projects should always be measured *after* blocking unless otherwise specified.

To measure the gauge of a lace pattern stitch:

1. Cast on the number of stitches called for in the pattern-stitch repeat, plus two extra stitches to create smooth edges.
2. Knit at least one full repeat of the pattern between the two extra stitches. Knit the extra edge stitches on every row.

Yarn Weights

Craft Yarn Council of America yarn standards don't account for the threadlike lace and cobweb-weight yarns that are often used for lace, so I've included all these in the super-fine category. Check the yarn requirements carefully if you substitute a different yarn for a project. Compare both the yardage and weight of the yarn to the yarn that I used to make sure you're choosing a suitable replacement. When in doubt, ask the helpful staff of your local yarn shop.

Yarn-Weight Symbol and Category Names	Super Fine 🧶1	Fine 🧶2	Light 🧶3	Medium 🧶4	Bulky 🧶5	Super Bulky 🧶6
Types of Yarns in Category	Sock, Fingering, Baby	Sport, Baby	DK, Light Worsted	Worsted, Afghan, Aran	Chunky, Craft, Rug	Bulky, Roving
Knit Gauge Ranges in Stockinette Stitch to 4"	27 to 32 sts	23 to 26 sts	21 to 24 sts	16 to 20 sts	12 to 15 sts	6 to 11 sts
Recommended Needle in Metric Size Range	2.25 to 3.25 mm	3.25 to 3.75 mm	3.75 to 4.5 mm	4.5 to 5.5 mm	5.5 to 8 mm	8 mm and larger
Recommended Needle in U.S. Size Range	1 to 3	3 to 5	5 to 7	7 to 9	9 to 11	11 and larger

3. Block your swatch (see page 9 for blocking instructions).

4. Place a rustproof pin at each end of your swatch, inside the edge stitches, and measure the number of inches between the pins.

- If this number is larger than the given gauge, your gauge is too loose. Try again, using a smaller needle.

- If this number is smaller than the given gauge, your gauge is too tight. Try again, using a larger needle.

Although exact gauge is not critical for shawls and scarves, and it can be difficult to measure gauge precisely on the soft, stretchy lace stitches, don't skip making a gauge swatch! When I first started, I thought a circle is a circle is a circle and did not give gauge instructions to my first test knitter. She created a lovely, tightly knit cape, but definitely not the full circle I'd expected. Working the gauge swatch also lets you practice the lace stitches in your project, so you can make mistakes in your swatch instead of in your scarf or shawl.

Yarn Overs

Yarn overs form the holes that make lace knitting lacy. A yarn over is shown as a circle on a chart and is abbreviated YO in written instructions.

A yarn over is made by wrapping the yarn around the needle; from which direction depends on the next stitch coming up on the left needle.

- If the stitch after the yarn over is a knit stitch, wrap across the front so that the yarn is right there ready for the next knit stitch.

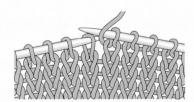

Yarn over between knits

- If the stitch after the yarn over is a purl stitch, a yarn over takes two motions rather than one. If the yarn is in the back, bring it to the front

between the needles. Wrap the yarn around the needle in a counterclockwise motion, moving up across the front of the needle and then down across the back of the needle. Bring the yarn to the front between the two needles to purl the next stitch.

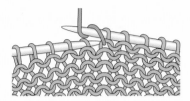

Yarn over between purls

When you're working a wrong-side row and come to a yarn over, put the right needle into the space of that yarn over and purl it as a stitch. Don't twist the thing to make a nice, neat stitch the same size as the others, as I did as a newbie with no idea. You want that open space.

Decreases

Every time you work a yarn over, you increase by adding a new stitch to your knitting. To keep the number of stitches constant throughout the pattern, you pair these yarn overs with different types of decreases. Sometimes each yarn over is matched to a decrease on the same row of knitting. In more complex lace patterns, decreases may fall several rows after the yarn over, causing the stitch count to vary throughout the pattern.

KNIT DECREASES

The basic decreases, knit-two-together (K2tog) and slip-slip-knit (ssk), slant in opposite directions and balance each other out, both visually and so that the lace doesn't develop a bias in the fabric.

To K2tog, simply knit two stitches together as if they were one.

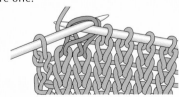

To work an ssk, slip the next stitch onto the right needle as if to knit it, do so again with the stitch after that, and then put the left needle into the fronts of the two stitches and knit them together that way.

Move two slipped stitches to left needle.

Knit the two stitches together.

PURL DECREASES

On the more challenging patterns, yarn overs and decreases are worked on both right-side and wrong-side rows, requiring you to decrease while purling. Just as K2tog and ssk slant in opposite directions and balance each other out, so do purl two together (P2tog) and purl two together through the back loops (P2tog-tbl). You can see the effect of the decrease slanting in the way the stems of the flowers of Wanda's Flowers Shawl on page 29 gracefully turn in continuous curves.

To P2tog, work two purl stitches together as if they were one.

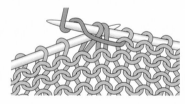

To P2tog-tbl, insert the right needle through two purl stitches through the back of the loops from left to right. Purl the two stitches together.

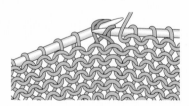

DOUBLE DECREASES

A double decrease removes two stitches at once and is often used between two yarn overs. On a right-side row, the most common double decreases in lace knitting are sl 1-K2tog-psso and sl 2-K1-p2sso. I find that the latter decrease takes an extra motion and

extra time to knit, but it makes for a crisper point at the top of the arrow-shaped decrease. Sometimes that matters; sometimes it doesn't. I used both of these double decreases throughout the book, so read the lace instructions and charts carefully to make sure you are working the correct version.

To work sl 1-K2tog-psso, slip one stitch knitwise onto the right needle, knit the next two stitches together, then pass the slipped stitch back over the one stitch you've just made.

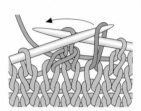

Slip one stitch as if to knit. Knit the next two stitches together.

Pass the slipped stitch over the knit stitch on the right needle.

To work sl 2-K1-p2sso, slip two stitches, knit one, then slip both of the slipped stitches back over the one.

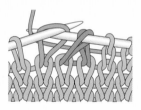
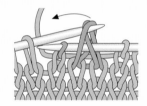

Slip two stitches together as if to knit. Knit the next stitch on the left needle.

Pass the two slipped stitches over the knit stitch on the right.

Joining a New Ball of Yarn

To join a new ball, I divide the plies of the yarn ends, from both my working yarn and the new ball, back to about a distance of 4" or 5". Then I break off one strand if it's a two- or three-ply, two if it's a four-ply, and follow the twist of the yarn in tightly wrapping those now-thinner ends back around each other. If it's not a Superwash wool or silk yarn (that is, if it's an animal fiber with some feltability), I dampen the joined piece, rub my fingers over it vigorously, and roll it between my hands to encourage the fibers to lock together. If it is silk or Superwash, I'll often make a longer join of 6" or 7".

If you find a knot in the yarn as you are knitting, cut it open and join as above.

Lifelines

A lifeline is a thread run through the loops across a row in knitted lace that gives you a way to easily rip out your knitting if you find a mistake, without risking having multiple stitches run as you frog (see "Terms and Abbreviations" on page 78 for a definition). By the time I'd heard of this wonderful idea, I was past the point where I really needed it, but it would have been helpful earlier in my lace-learning curve, so I offer it here. To create a lifeline, thread a sewing needle and run it through all the stitches on the needle every now and then. Dental floss works well. When frogging, once you reach the lifeline, you can simply slip the stitches back onto your needle and go on. A lifeline may also make it easier to catch and recover an individual dropped stitch.

Charts or Written Instructions?

In this book, I've provided both charts and written instructions for the lace patterns. I knit from the written instructions, but I know that many knitters prefer knitting from charts. Whichever you prefer, you will get the same results. Don't try to match them up, however. The repeats on charts are made to be nice, tidy rectangles, while the repeats in the text are made to limit the amount of counting, so they're not always the same. The actual knitting is the same; it's just the way the information is presented that is different.

Blocking

Blocking makes your knitted item match the dimensions specified in the pattern and finishes the texture of the knitting, smoothing out any inconsistencies in gauge. By stretching the knitting, the yarn overs open up, and the lace pattern becomes more visible and delicate.

To block a lace shawl or scarf:

1. Soak the finished item in lukewarm water with no soap until it is thoroughly wet.
2. Gently roll the item in a towel to remove excess water.
3. Lay the item out on a flat surface, such as a mattress or blocking board.
4. Run blocking wires through the stitches along the edges of the knitting, then use rustproof pins to secure the edges to the blocking surface.

5. Leave the scarf or shawl in place until it is thoroughly dry, at least 24 hours.

Top-Down Circular Shawls

All the shawls in this book are made using the same top-down construction. They are knitted back and forth but are shaped to form a circle that drapes beautifully over the shoulders when worn.

Basic Shape and Construction

To begin a circular shawl, you cast on only 12 to 15 stitches, then increase to double the number of stitches several times. If you want a wider neck for wearing the shawl thrown over the shoulder more loosely at the top, begin with the stitch count listed after the first increase row. Depending on the number of increases, the shawl may form a half circle, full circle, or ruffled shape that is larger than a circle.

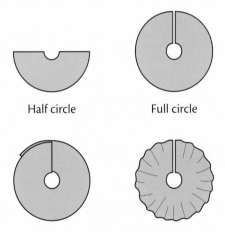

Half circle   Full circle

More than a full circle

After the first sets of increases are complete, you work a yoke pattern. You then double the number of stitches again and work the remainder of the shawl body in the main pattern stitch. In a few of the shawls, I've included a border pattern at the bottom edge.

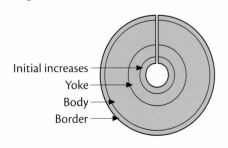

Initial increases
Yoke
Body
Border

NECK EDGES

To make the neck edge stronger and because it makes the shawl look prettier and feel softer against the neck, I suggest casting on with a double strand of yarn. Cut the extra strand after completing the cast on, leaving a tail at least 12" long. Weave the ends in as you purl the first row (or, if you prefer, weave in the ends after you finish knitting the shawl). You can weave in the two tail strands as you purl, or you can weave them in after the knitting is complete.

To keep the cast-on edge very loose, I cast on a stitch, push it back about 1" from the tip of the needle, and hold it back there without letting it become too taut while casting on the next stitch.

SIZES

Each scarf and shawl in this book can be made any length you like. I've included some guidelines and notes about the sizes that I made, but these are approximate figures, because the knitted lace fabric is very stretchy. If you lay a shawl on a table and measure the length, it may be 19", and when you drape it over your shoulders, it may stretch to as much as 22" as the fabric drapes around your body. You should feel free to make each item the size that feels comfortable to you. Just remember that if you add much in length or width, you will need to purchase extra yarn!

Changing the length of a shawl is easy; just knit until it is as long as you want. You can also change the look of a shawl by changing the width. If you knit one shawl with fewer stitches and one shawl with more stitches and make them the same length, you will see that the narrower garment fits like a fitted cape while the looser garment is a flowing shawl.

DESIGNING YOUR OWN
TOP-DOWN CIRCULAR SHAWL

After you knit one or two shawls in this easy shape, you will want to design your own. Be careful which combinations of stitches you put together. If you have a pattern that is, say, 6 stitches per repeat across, then below that, you put one that is 10 stitches across, they will not flow naturally into each other if you double the number of stitches for the lower section. I tried it once, early on, just to see, and immediately frogged

it. When the patterns chosen have the same number of stitches or are even multiples of the same number—6 and 12, 8 and 16; or 6 and 6, 8 and 8, for example—it works out beautifully. I did do one design where I didn't quite double the number of stitches in the final increase row, wanting to put two patterns together that were not in matching multiples, and it worked.

When a pattern is a repeat of, say 6 + 1 stitches, and the pattern to be used above or below it is a repeat of 6 + 4 stitches, those 3 extra stitches need to be added at the end of the row, not divided up evenly across the row. Don't try to center the second pattern within the overall shawl, or the up-and-down flow of the patterns will be off by a noticeable jog. This does mean one edge of the shawl will go outward just a bit on those longer rows, which, in the bottom section, would actually be a plus as you wear the shawl draped back over your shoulder.

Choosing yarn and colors for your own designs is an adventure as well, as you will learn in several of the stories scattered throughout this book. The weight and fiber of the yarn you choose will determine whether your finished garment is airy or fluffy as well as whether it is stretchy or firm. If you can't find a yarn in the exact color you see in your mind's eye, consider overdyeing the yarn yourself. Your local yarn store will most likely have all the supplies and instructions you need, or they can order them.

These overdyed yarns all began as the light blue in the center.

Nina's Story

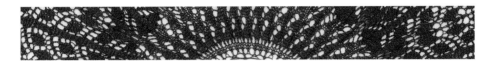

$\mathcal{V}$IRGINIA WAS ASKING ME, "Do you know how to sew this kind of fabric?" Slippery and synthetic, and no, I didn't have a clue.

Nina had been a music major in college at Ann Arbor, then moved to Boston, where she'd met Virginia. Now Virginia, my neighbor, was looking forward to rejoicing with her old friend Nina at her good fortune at finding Rod. If she could just get this matron of honor dress done and keep her little Daniel from climbing down the laundry chute in the meantime. Oh, great, now he's washing his hair with toothpaste! "Whatja do, use half the tube?"

I tried my best to help with the dress, but ended up picking up the undone mending in the corner and doing that instead. The worst drudge jobs don't seem like drudgery when they're somebody else's.

Three years later, my husband and I found ourselves moving to Nina's town. We'd never laid eyes on Nina or Rod, and yet the fact that we were Virginia's friends was good enough for them. They offered us dinner on moving day. I was so glad. Cooking was the last thing on earth I wanted to do. They were perfectly understanding of our being delayed with the movers and of having to clean up our baby, who'd crawled into the fireplace and gleefully played in the soot when I wasn't paying attention. Daniel would have been proud of her. Now where did that box of baby clothes end up!

It wasn't just any dinner: it was Nina's first attempt at doing a Seder. Nina's grandparents had fled the Nazis in Austria; she wanted to connect to her roots and honor her ancestors by commemorating the Passover. To welcome the strangers at the gates—us.

We've been close friends for 18 years as I write this. It all began with that dinner. Nina recently took up knitting again for the first time since she was a teenager, using the orange straight needles with hot pink flowers painted on the ends she'd gotten in 1969. Go Flower Power.

You know I had to make Nina one of these shawls. In an arbor pattern, to match not only where she went to school but also her stage name as a DJ at the community college radio station where she has the wonderful chance to play an eclectic mix of music from superb but undiscovered talent. Let's welcome—Ann Arbor!

And if I ever meet Daniel's young bride someday, I'll make her a scarf, but you know what the lace pattern would have to be? *"Crest" of the Wave*. In mint.

Nina's Ann Arbor Shawl

This is a generous, sweeping shawl,
good for tossing over the shoulder and
showing off a beautiful shawl pin.

Materials

- 🌀 8 skeins of 100% Alpaca from Pacific Meadows Alpaca (150 yds per skein) in color Light Blue **🔳3**
- 🌀 Size 9 (5.5 mm) circular needle, 32" to 40" long, or size to obtain gauge
- 🌀 Size 13 (9 mm) knitting needle for binding off
- 🌀 Tapestry needle for weaving in tails

Note: *I bought a 1,800-yd/450-g cone, made my own hank, and washed and dyed the yarn. I used 9.5 oz for this shawl.*

Skill Level

◼◼◼▭
Intermediate

Finished Blocked Measurements

Length: Approx 24½"
Bottom Circumference: Approx 168"

Gauge

20-st rep = 8" over body pattern
(chart B or rows 30–39), blocked

Instructions

CO 14 sts loosely, doubling yarn for the CO row and keeping sts at least 1" apart (see "Neck Edges" on page 10).

Row 1 (RS): K1, (YO, K1) across—27 sts.

Row 2 (WS): Purl.

Row 3: (YO, K1) across—54 sts.

Row 4: Purl.

Row 5: (K1, YO) across, end K1—107 sts.

Row 6: Purl.

Row 7: Knit.

Row 8: Purl.

Row 9: (K1, YO) across, end K2—212 sts.

YOKE

Worked over a multiple of 5 + 2 sts. St count varies from row to row. See chart A on page 14 for rows 10–15 if you prefer to work from charts.

Row 10 (WS): K2, *P3, K2; rep from *.

Row 11 (RS): P2, *K3, YO, P2; rep from *.

Row 12: K2, *P4, K2; rep from *.

Row 13: P2, *K1, K2tog, YO, K1, P2; rep from *.

Row 14: K2, *P2, P2tog, K2; rep from *.

Row 15: P2, *K1, YO, K2tog, P2; rep from *.

Rows 16–27: Rep rows 10–15 twice more.

Row 28: Rep row 10.

Row 29: K1, (K1, YO) across, end K2—421 sts.

BODY

Worked over a multiple of 20 + 1 sts. St count varies from row to row. See chart B below for rows 30–39 if you prefer to work from charts.

Row 30 (and all WS rows through row 38): Purl.

Row 31 (RS): *K1, ssk, YO, K5, (YO, K1) 5 times, YO, K5, YO, K2tog; rep from *, end K1.

Row 33: *K1, ssk, YO, ssk, K1, (K2tog, YO) twice, K3, YO, K1, YO, K3, (YO, ssk) twice, K1, K2tog, YO, K2tog; rep from *, end K1.

Row 35: *K1, ssk, YO, sl 2-K1-P2sso, YO, K2tog, YO, K5, YO, K1, YO, K5, YO, ssk, YO, sl 2-K1-P2sso, YO, K2tog; rep from *, end K1.

Row 37: *K1, sl 1-K2tog-psso, YO, K2tog, YO, K1, YO, ssk, K1, K2tog, YO, sl 2-K1-P2sso, YO, ssk, K1, K2tog, YO, K1, YO, ssk, YO, K3tog; rep from * to last st, K1.

Row 39: *K2, K2tog, YO, K3, (YO, sl 2-K1-P2sso) 3 times, YO, K3, YO, ssk, K1; rep from *, end K1.

Rep rows 30–39 until shawl measures approx 24½" long and body pattern has been worked 5 times.

BOTTOM EDGE

Next row (WS): Purl.

Next row (RS): (K2tog, YO) across, end K1.

Next row (WS): Purl.

BO loosely, using size 13 needle. Weave in tails and block.

Body pattern

Chart A Yoke

Starts on row 10 (WS).

Key

☐ K on RS, P on WS	╱ K2tog
● P on RS, K on WS	⊡ P2tog
▨ No stitch	⧅ sl 2-K1-p2sso
⊙ YO	⧄ sl 1-K2tog-psso
╲ ssk	╱ K3tog

Pattern rep   End sts

Chart B Body

Starts on row 30 (WS).

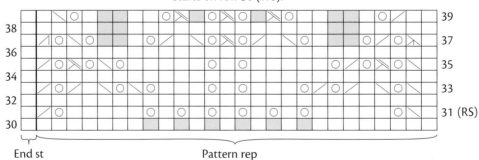

End st   Pattern rep

Kathy's Story

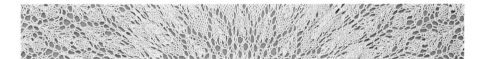

I WAS DOODLING, drawing a heron, so unwittingly like the ones I'd drawn as a kid that it startled me. Why did that look so extremely familiar? Then I remembered—and wondered how this drawing had come out of my pencil just as if I'd photocopied it from my childhood.

I had a very best friend all through elementary school. Kathy was funny, way cuter than I was—I thought it would be so cool to have gorgeous, long blonde hair, too—and she got along with everybody. We were inseparable.

But in fourth grade, disaster struck. My mother, instead of signing me up for Girl Scouts so I could go do cool stuff with Kathy, signed me up for piano lessons. When the demanding teacher required I attend two lessons a week, one with a buddy, one with a larger group, there went any chance of Girl Scouts. My grandmother was in on it, too. She was a former music professor, and she'd picked out my teacher herself, one that had a chance of turning me into a professional someday. Yes, I wanted to learn piano, but . . . crum.

I showed up that first week excited but nervous as all get-out. Till I walked in the door on that first group-lesson day—Kathy was there! Our mothers immediately had us reassigned as buddies so they could carpool both days. Of all the piano teachers in the entire Maryland suburbs of DC, how Kathy's folks had picked the same one, a half hour from home, I have never known. But there we were. And so our lives continued in lockstep as best friends.

One of my happy memories is of picking clover flowers together at recess, slitting a hole in the stems with our fingernails, threading another stem through, till we had flower necklaces—keeping the sweet smell of recess and grass and blue skies wrapped around us as we went back to our desks.

In seventh grade, Kathy and her family moved to New Mexico, and the pictures she sent of the desert matched how it felt with her gone. A few years later, she was writing from California. Her dad had died in an accident and her mom had gone back to school. We managed to connect a few more times over the years, but by now it's been ages.

Kathy, if you read this, I have your purple clover shawl here. Stop by during recess sometime. I've got Gram's piano now, so we can sit down and play our favorite "Dancing Sergeants" duet. You'd be surprised at how the muscle memory will still be right there in those hands.

Postscript: I found her! She has and treasures her shawl. And it all started with that doodle.

Kathy's Clover-Chain Shawl

This clover stitch would make a good pattern for a stole, too, because the up-and-down direction is not as obvious as in some patterns. For a rectangular stole, cast on an odd-numbered multiple of 10 + 1 sts—such as 31, 51, or 71—and simply work rows 30–56 for the desired length.

Materials

- ⚭ 6 skeins of 100% Alpaca from Pacific Meadows Alpaca (150 yds per skein) in color Light Pink
- ⚭ Size 9 (5.5 mm) circular needle, 32" to 40" long, or size to obtain gauge
- ⚭ Size 13 (9 mm) knitting needle for binding off
- ⚭ Tapestry needle for weaving in tails

Note: I bought a 1,800-yd/450-g cone, made my own hank, washed the yarn, and then overdyed the original Light Pink with a small amount of purple Jacquard acid dye to get the shade for this shawl. I used 6.8 oz of yarn.

Skill Level

■■■▢

Intermediate

Finished Blocked Measurements

Length: Approx 22"
Bottom Circumference: Approx 123½"

Gauge

10-st rep = 3¼" over body pattern (chart B or rows 30–57), blocked

Instructions

CO 12 sts loosely, doubling yarn for the CO row and keeping sts at least 1" apart (see "Neck Edges" on page 10).

Row 1 (and all WS rows): Purl.

Row 2: (YO, K1) across—24 sts.

Row 4: (YO, K1) across—48 sts.

Row 6: K2, *K2tog, YO, K1; rep from *, end K1.

Row 8: K2, *YO, K1, K2tog; rep from *, end K1.

Row 10: (YO, K1) across—96 sts.

Row 12: Rep row 6.

Row 14: Rep row 8.

Row 16: Rep row 6.

Row 18: (K1, YO) across, end K1—191 sts.

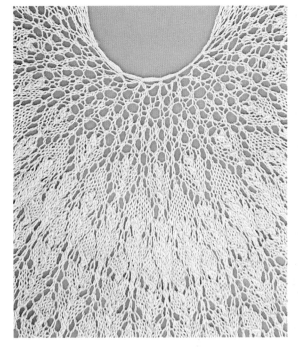

Yoke pattern

YOKE

Worked over a multiple of 10 + 1 sts. See chart A on page 19 for rows 20–27 if you prefer working from charts. Cont purling all WS rows.

Row 20 (RS): K1, *YO, K3, sl 1-K2tog-psso, K3, YO, K1; rep from *.

Row 22: K1, *K1, YO, K2, sl 1-K2tog-psso, K2, YO, K2; rep from *.

Row 24: K1, *K2, YO, K1, sl 1-K2tog-psso, K1, YO, K3; rep from *.

Row 26: K1, *K3, YO, sl 1-K2tog-psso, YO, K4; rep from *.

Row 28: (K1, YO) across, end K1—381 sts.

Row 29: Purl.

BODY

Worked over a multiple of 10 + 1 sts. See chart B on page 19 for rows 30–57 if you prefer working from charts. Cont purling all WS rows.

Row 30 (RS): (Ssk) twice, *(YO, K1) 3 times, YO, K2tog, sl 1-K2tog-psso, ssk; rep from *, end last rep (K2tog) twice.

Row 32: Ssk, *K3, YO, K1, YO, K3, sl 1-K2tog-psso; rep from *, end last rep K2tog.

Row 34: Ssk, *K2, YO, K3, YO, K2, sl 1-K2tog-psso; rep from *, end last rep K2tog.

Row 36: Ssk, *K1, YO, K5, YO, K1, sl 1-K2tog-psso; rep from *, end last rep K2tog.

Row 38: Ssk, *YO, K1, YO, ssk, K1, K2tog, YO, K1, YO, sl 1-K2tog-psso; rep from *, end last rep K2tog.

Row 40: Ssk, *YO, K2, YO, sl 1-K2tog-psso; rep from *, end last rep K2tog.

Row 42: K1, *YO, K3, sl 1-K2tog-psso, K3, YO, K1; rep from *.

Row 44: K1, *YO, K1, YO, K2tog, sl 1-K2tog-psso, ssk, (YO, K1) twice; rep from *.

Row 46: Rep row 42.

Row 48: K2, *YO, K2, sl 1-K2tog-psso, K2, YO, K3; rep from *, end last rep K2.

Row 50: K3, *YO, K1, sl 1-K2tog-psso, K1, YO, K5; rep from *, end last rep K3.

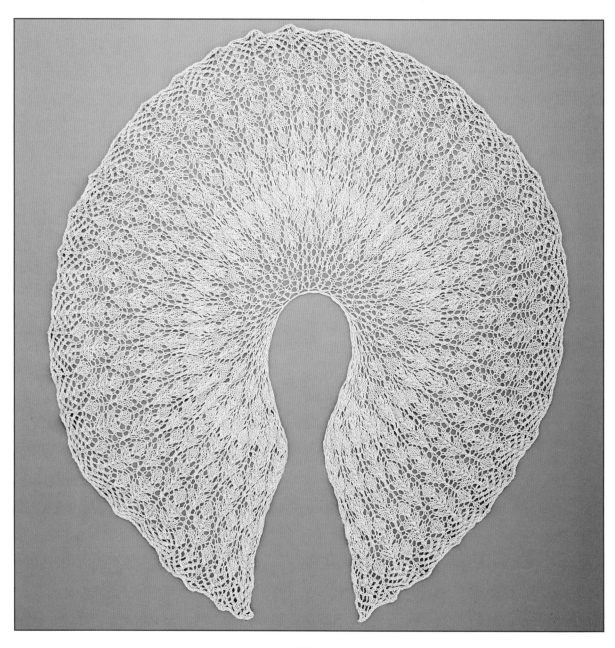

Row 52: K1, *K2tog, YO, K1, YO, sl 1-K2tog-psso, YO, K1, YO, ssk, K1; rep from *.

Row 54: Rep row 40.

Row 56: Rep row 32.

Row 57: Purl.

Rows 58–85: Rep rows 30–57.

BOTTOM EDGE

Row 86 (RS): K1, *(YO, ssk) twice, K1, (K2tog, YO) twice, K1; rep from *.

Rows 87 and 89 (WS): Purl.

Row 88: K2, *YO, ssk, YO, sl 1-K2tog-psso, YO, K2tog, YO, K3; rep from *, end last rep K2.

Row 89 (WS): Purl.

Rows 90–97: Rep rows 86–89 twice more.

BO loosely, using size 13 needle. Weave in tails and block.

Body pattern and bottom edge

Chart A Yoke
Starts on row 20 (RS).

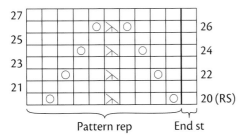

Pattern rep   End st

Key

☐ K on RS, P on WS
⊡ YO
◹ ssk
◺ K2tog
⧄ sl 1-K2tog-psso

Chart B Body
Starts on row 30 (RS).

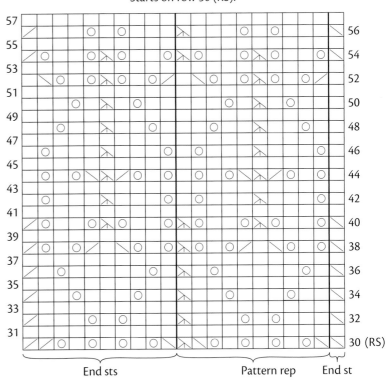

End sts   Pattern rep   End st

Concert Story

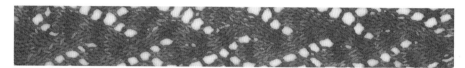

$\mathcal{L}$OVING GOOD music, but being hearing impaired, I arrived early for the concert at my church so that I could sit near the front. Karen Bentley Pollick is a superb violinist who has performed extensively professionally, but this night she was to play simply for the love of it because an old friend of hers, Russ, had asked if she would while she was in town.

I found myself chatting with a man who, I soon discovered, was Karen's fiancé. A woman, Karen herself it turned out, joined us before going onstage.

Wanting to thank her afterward, I knitted her a baby alpaca lace scarf. She had given freely, and freely she would receive. Having no idea where she lived or whether she'd even want a complete stranger to know, I asked Russ, who mailed it off for me.

The next summer, I was hospitalized at Stanford. While critically ill, I heard beautiful harp music playing. I wondered wistfully which patient had someone love them so much that they would bring a harp there to play for them. I tried to picture it squeezed between the beds and quite wished someone would want to do that for me.

Eight months later, Ms. Pollick was back in town and word came from Russ that she would be playing with her friends in the atrium at Stanford, part of an ongoing series of free concerts for the benefit of the patients and public.

So that's why I'd heard that harp music! I looked up the series and found that, yes, a harpist had often been there. Oh!

I sent off an email to Ms. Pollick to let her know that I would be coming to the concert. She was delighted at the chance to say thank you in person for her scarf. But when it came down to it, I discovered later, she really wasn't sure she would recognize me. After all, there hadn't been anything much to stick me in her memory at the time I'd talked with her, given that she'd had no idea then what she'd be getting out of the deal.

I set off for Stanford. As I walked down the stairs to the atrium, she saw my long lace scarf hanging, caught my eye and nodded, affirming. "Yes. That's her."

I watched preoccupied people passing by on the floors above suddenly stop to listen. The music was beautiful.

Afterward, I thanked the musicians and told them that from the point of view of a patient, what they were doing was absolutely essential. Knowing somebody was performing for the sake of blessing others, when the alternative was to lie there listening to one's IV drip. . . . There are no words to describe how much their gifts lift one's spirits. Exactly the effect they had hoped for.

Concert Scarf

This is adapted from Barbara Walker's Grapevine Trellis
pattern and is done with two repeats: one-half of the beginning
and ending repeats each forms a frame to the interior. Widen by
adding multiples of 12 stitches if desired.

Materials

- ❀ 2 balls of Fine Cashmere from Tess' Designer Yarns (100% cashmere; 245 yds; 50 g per ball) in color Natural
- ❀ Size 11 (8 mm) needles or size to obtain gauge
- ❀ Tapestry needle for weaving in tails

Skill Level

■■■☐
Intermediate

Finished Blocked Measurements

Length: 72"
Width: 9"

Gauge

36 sts = 9" over pattern stitch (chart or rows 6–17)

Instructions

CO 36 sts.

BEGINNING BORDER

Row 1 (and all WS rows): Purl.

Row 2: (K2tog, YO) across, end K2.

Row 4: Knit.

Row 5: Purl.

MAIN PATTERN

Worked over a multiple of 12 + 6 sts. St count varies from row to row. See chart on page 23 for rows 6–17 if you prefer to work from charts. Cont to purl WS rows.

Row 6 (RS): K2, YO, K2tog, K1, *K2tog, K1, (YO, ssk) twice, YO, K1, ssk, K2; rep from * to last 7 sts, end K3, ssk, YO, K2.

Row 8: K2, YO, (K2tog) twice, K1, YO, *K1, (YO, ssk) twice, YO, K1, ssk, K2tog, K1, YO; rep from *, end K1, ssk, YO, K2.

Row 10: K2, YO, K2tog, K2, YO, *K3, (YO, ssk) twice, YO, K1, ssk, K1, YO; rep from *, end K2, ssk, YO, K2.

Row 12: K2, YO, K2tog, K4, *K2tog, K1, YO, (K2tog, YO) twice, K1, ssk, K2; rep from *, end K1, ssk, YO, K2.

Row 14: K2, YO, K2tog, K3, *K2tog, K1, YO, (K2tog, YO) twice, K1, YO, K1, ssk; rep from *, end K2, ssk, YO, K2.

Row 16: K2, YO, K2tog, K2, K2tog, *K1, YO, (K2tog, YO) twice, K3, YO, K1, K2tog; rep from *, end K1, ssk, YO, K2.

Row 17: Purl.

Rep rows 6–17 until scarf is 72" or desired length.

END BORDER

Cont to purl WS rows.

Next RS row: Rep row 4.

Next RS row: Rep row 2.

Next row (WS): Purl.

BO all sts. Weave in tails and block.

Scarf Chart

Starts on row 6 (RS).

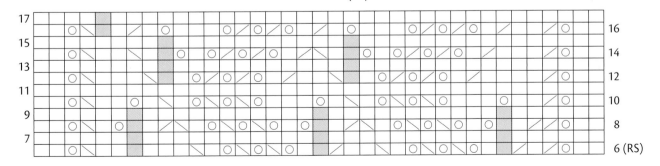

Key

☐ K on RS, P on WS

◯ YO

◣ ssk

◢ K2tog

▨ No stitch

Zinnia Story

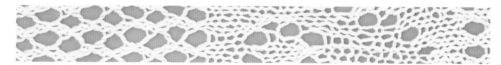

"*IF YOU GO TO SAN FRANCISCO,* be sure to wear some flowers in your hair. . . ."

Michelle glanced in my mirror from the hallway. She stopped dead in her tracks, horrified. "Promise me you're not going to wear that flower on your head!" she wailed. I grinned the delightfully malicious grin of a parent who has successfully mortified her teenager and said, "Oh yes!"

We were flying east that morning for our older daughter's wedding reception. Four months earlier, I'd been sitting in a lecture during which the speaker had handed a tiny plastic pot to everyone. The cliché of a bean in the soil for kindergarten class? She said, "Add water and find out."

"I'm game," I thought, and took it home and set it under the skylight in the bathroom. As soon as the first true leaves appeared, I was delighted to discover: zinnias!

They wanted more light. They grew leggy. Would they bloom? And then finally the first orange flower opened, regardless of sun or size, on the morning we were to leave town for that reception.

I couldn't stand it. I just couldn't leave it there to die unappreciated. I did my hair back in a French roll, thought about it, picked that little flower waving on its spindly stalk, and stuck it on my head, secured by the twist in my hair. It waved like a small single-antenna deely-bopper.

Airports and I just weren't made for each other. I crossed the airport in a wheelchair, which meant my face and my flower and I were at eye level with the four-year-old girl who'd come to wave good-bye to her mommy. She thought that a real flower stuck in one's hair waving around was the coolest thing she'd ever seen in her life. We were instant friends. And I was getting on the same flight as her mother. That made it not so bad, because her mommy wouldn't have to go alone.

…And the copilot of the plane came up behind me as he strode briskly toward our gate, and as he passed, he brushed a hand lightly on my shoulder and smiled back at me, "Nice flower."

…And the flight attendants all came over and talked about zinnias and knitting with me.

…And every person who noticed that flower and my willingness to make light of myself with it brightened a little, and whether they said anything directly to me or not, went on their way a little happier.

Be sure to wear some flowers, wherever you're flying off to. If your hair's too busy, here's my knitted version to wear or to wrap around someone you love.

Zinnia Scarf

For the simplest lace pattern, one that will stretch a small
amount of a premium yarn a long way, cast on an odd number
of stitches and do just rows 30 and 32 to the length desired. It looks
beautiful in both fuzzy and plain yarns. The instructions given here
are for the warm and fluffy red version.

Materials

- 1 skein of Suri Dream by Knitpicks
  (74% Suri alpaca, 22% wool, 4% nylon;
  50 g; 143 yds per skein) in color Strawberry
  Z773
- Size 10½ (6.5 mm) needles or size to
  obtain gauge
- Tapestry needle for weaving in tails

Skill Level

◖■■□
Intermediate

Finished Blocked Measurements

Length: 52"
Width: 8"

Gauge

19 sts = 8" over body pattern (chart A or rows 30–33),
blocked

Instructions

CO 19 sts.

TOP BORDER

See chart A on page 27 for rows 1–29 if you prefer to
work from charts.

Row 1 (and WS rows unless otherwise specified): Purl.

Row 2: (K2tog, YO) across, end K1.

Rows 4 and 6: Knit.

Row 8: K3, K2tog, K4, YO, P1, YO, K4, ssk, K3.

Rows 9, 11, 13, 15, and 17: P9, K1, P9.

Row 10: K3, K2tog, K3, YO, K1, P1, K1, YO, K3, ssk, K3.

Row 12: K3, K2tog, K2, YO, K2, P1, K2, YO, K2, ssk, K3.

Row 14: K3, K2tog, K1, YO, K3, P1, K3, YO, K1, ssk, K3.

Row 16: K3, K2tog, YO, K4, P1, K4, YO, ssk, K3.

Row 18: K7, K2tog, YO, P1, YO, ssk, K7.

Row 19 (and every WS row hereafter until bottom border): Purl.

Row 20: K6, K2tog, YO, K3, YO, ssk, K6.

Row 22: K6, ssk, YO, K3, YO, K2tog, K6.

Row 24: K8, YO, sl 1-K2tog-psso, YO, K8.

Rows 26 and 28: Knit.

Row 29 (WS): Purl.

SCARF CENTER

See chart A on page 27 for rows 30–33 if you prefer
working from charts. Cont to purl WS rows.

Row 30 (RS): K1, (K2tog, YO) across, end K2.

Row 32: K2, (YO, ssk) across, end K1.

Row 33 (WS): Purl.

Repeat rows 30–33 until scarf is desired length minus
the bottom flower section.

BOTTOM BORDER

See chart B on page 27 for rows 1–29 if you prefer
working from charts. Cont to purl WS rows unless
otherwise specified.

Rows 1, 3, and 5 (WS): Purl.

Rows 2 and 4 (RS): Knit.

Row 6: K7, K2tog, YO, P1, YO, ssk, K7.

Row 8: K6, K2tog, YO, K3, YO, ssk, K6.

Row 10: K6, ssk, YO, K3, YO, K2tog, K6.

Row 12: K8, YO, sl 1-K2tog-psso, YO, K8.

Rows 13, 15, 17, 19, and 21: P9, K1, P9.

Row 14: K3, ssk, YO, K4, P1, K4, YO, K2tog, K3.

Row 16: K3, ssk, K1, YO, K3, P1, K3, YO, K1, K2tog, K3.

Row 18: K3, ssk, K2, YO, K2, P1, K2, YO, K2, K2tog, K3.

Row 20: K3, ssk, K3, YO, K1, P1, K1, YO, K3, K2tog, K3.

Row 22: K3, ssk, K4, YO, P1, YO, K4, K2tog, K3.

Rows 24 and 26: Knit.

Row 28: (K2tog, YO) across, end K1.

Row 29 (WS): Purl.

BO all sts. Weave in tails and block.

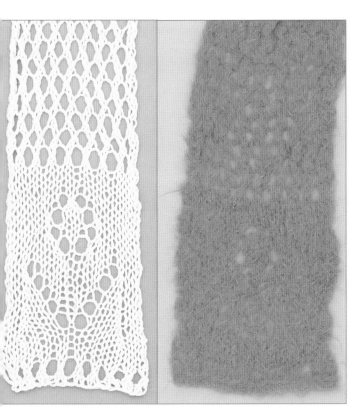

Left: The Zinnia Scarf made in Rowan Soft Baby yarn.
Right: The Zinnia Scarf made in Suri Dream by
Knitpicks, in color Strawberry 2773.

Chart A Top Border
Starts on row 1 (WS).
Center starts on row 30.

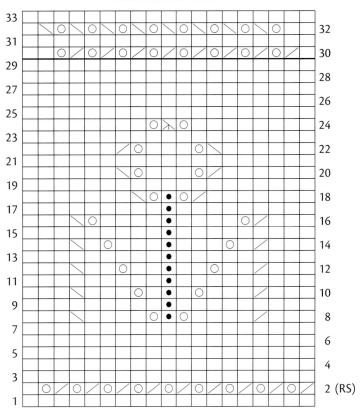

Chart B Bottom Border
Starts on row 1 (WS).

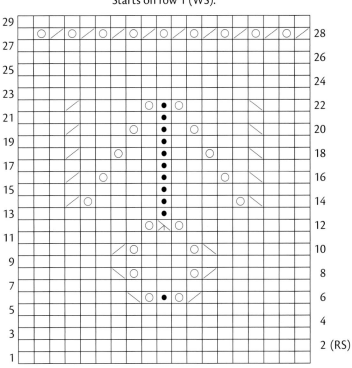

Key
- ☐ K on RS, P on WS
- ● P on RS, K on WS
- ⊙ YO
- ◻ ssk
- ◻ K2tog
- ⊠ sl 1-K2tog-psso

Wanda's Story

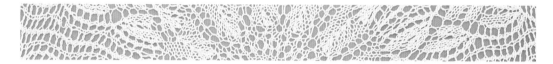

WE WERE NEW HOMEOWNERS with two toddlers in New Hampshire. It was Easter Sunday, and Richard and I had prepared a feast of a meal. But something was missing.

Richard said, "We ought to invite Dave over to eat with us." Dave was Richard's office mate. My thought was, "Yeah, that would have been a good idea, but dinner will be ready in 10 minutes. Wouldn't it be rude to invite him now and have it look like an afterthought?"

Richard called anyway, affirming, "Dave's coming right over."

He was only 10 minutes away, and we had a grand time. After eating and after playing with our babies, Dave went to our piano and discovered how out of tune it was. Hey, he'd be delighted to fix that!

Whom you serve, you love.

That was how we all went from thinking well of each other to truly being friends. Which is why, when Dave married Wanda a few years after we'd moved to California and he'd moved home to Minnesota, he made a point of bringing his bride out to meet us.

Over the next several years, we prayed for Dave and Wanda during their long struggle with infertility. And then, the phone call came: Wanda was expecting triplets. There were problems, and they were calling old friends they knew they could count on to support them. We wept with them when their little Samuel didn't make it and rejoiced that Gregory and Mitchell did and were well. Pain and joy. So often so inseparable.

Dave and Wanda brought their sons out to see us just before the boys turned two. It was glorious, seeing those two so happy, having their hearts' desires: each other. Their babies. I found myself unexpectedly turning to Wanda, and saying out of the blue, "And maybe someday you'll have a girl."

The impact of that sentence! Goodness! Wanda turned to me with a look on her face I could only describe as amazed blissfulness, and said, thoughtfully, "Yeah . . . yeah. Maybe you're right."

Later, we found out they'd gone home and immediately called their clinic. They wanted to try again. They knew their chances were not very good. But soon we heard that Wanda was pregnant again, and the next Christmas, we received the most exquisite picture I've ever seen: the two boys were each holding a newborn sister on his lap. Each boy with a look on his face, turned to his brother, that exclaimed, "Oh my golly goodness. What are we in for now!"

I've always felt those were, somehow, my baby girls. They claimed my heart even before they were born.

Some people step into our lives only occasionally. But each time, it's as if there were no separation in between, because there is no separation of hearts. They are ours forever.

Wanda's Flowers Shawl

Barbara Walker's Dayflowers is one of the most graceful patterns in lace knitting. This uses one of the heavier-weight yarns in this book for a narrow shawl that works up quickly.

Materials

- ❧ 5 balls of Alpaca & Silk from Blue Sky Alpacas (50% alpaca 50% silk; 50 g; 146 yds per ball) in color I33 (**2**)
- ❧ Size 10 (6 mm) circular needle, 32" to 40" long, or size to obtain gauge
- ❧ Size 8 (5 mm) circular needle, 32" to 40" long
- ❧ Size 13 (9 mm) knitting needle for binding off
- ❧ Tapestry needle for weaving in tails

Skill Level

■■■◗

Experienced

Finished Blocked Measurements

Length: Approx 21"
Bottom Circumference: Approx 91"

Gauge

20-st rep = 7" over body pattern (chart B or rows 29–44), blocked

Instructions

Using size 8 needle, CO 10 sts loosely, doubling yarn for the CO row and keeping sts at least 1" apart (see "Neck Edges" on page 10).

Row 1 (RS): K1, (YO, K1) across—19 sts.

Row 2 (and all WS rows unless otherwise stated): Purl.

Row 3: K1, (YO, K1) across—37 sts.

Row 5: Knit.

Row 7: K2, (YO, K1) across—72 sts.

Change to size 10 needle.

Rows 9 and 13: K2, *K2tog, YO, K1, rep from *, end K1.

Row 11: K2, *YO, K1, K2tog, rep from *, end K1.

Row 15: K2, (YO, K1) across, end YO, K2—141 sts.

Row 16 (WS): Purl.

YOKE

Worked over a multiple of 10 + 1 sts. See chart A on page 32 for rows 17–26 if you prefer to work from charts.

Rows 17, 19, 21, 23, and 25 (RS): K1, *YO, K3, sl 1-K2tog-psso, K3, YO, K1; rep from *.

Row 18 (and all WS rows through row 26): Purl.

Row 27: K2, (YO, K1) across, end YO, K2—279 sts.

Row 28 (WS): Purl.

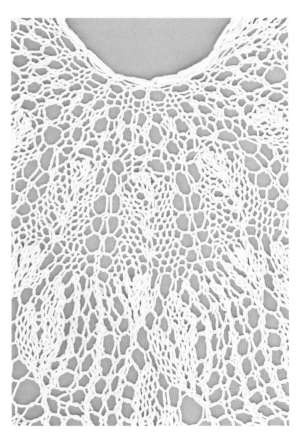

Yoke pattern

BODY

Worked over a multiple of 20 + 19 sts. St count varies from row to row. See chart B on page 32 for rows 29–44 if you prefer to work from charts.

Row 29 (RS): K2, YO, *K2tog, YO, (K2tog) 3 times, K2, YO, K3, YO, ssk, YO, K1, YO, sl 1-K2tog-psso, YO, K1, YO; rep from *, end last rep K2tog, YO, (K2tog) 3 times, K2, YO, K3, YO, ssk, YO, K2.

Row 30 (and all WS rows except 32 and 40): Purl.

Row 31: K2, YO, *K2tog, (K3tog) twice, YO, K1, YO, K2, (ssk, YO) twice, K1, YO, sl 1-K2tog-psso, YO, K1, YO; rep from *, end last rep K2 tog, (K3tog) twice, YO, K1, YO, K2, (ssk, YO) twice, K2.

Row 32 (WS): P11, *P2tog, P16; rep from * to last 6 sts, end P2 tog, P4.

Row 33: K2, YO, *K3tog, YO, K3, YO, K2, (ssk, YO) twice, K1, YO, sl 1-K2tog-psso, YO, K1, YO; rep from *, end last rep K3tog, YO, K3, YO, K2, (ssk, YO) twice, K2.

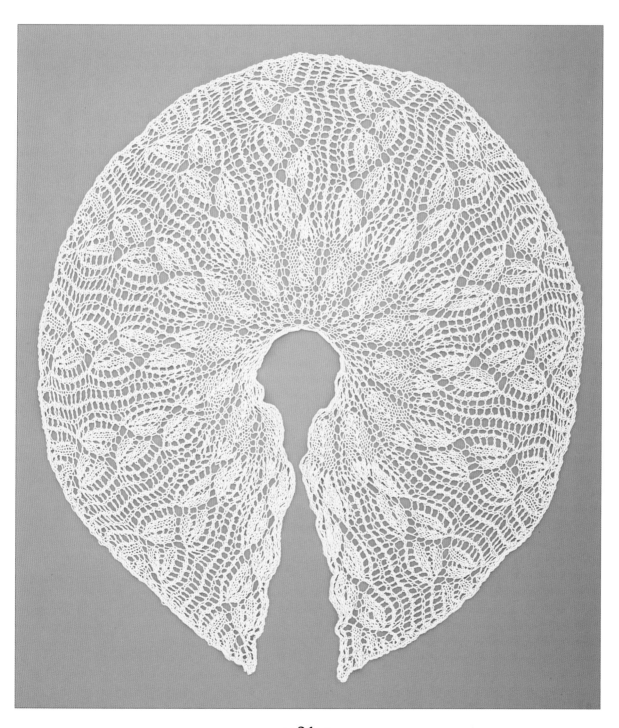

Row 35: K2, YO, *K2tog, YO, K1, (YO, K2, ssk) twice, YO, ssk, YO, K1, YO, sl 1-K2tog-psso, YO, K1, YO; rep from *, end last rep K2 tog, YO, K1, (YO, K2, ssk) twice, YO, ssk, YO, K2.

Row 37: K2, YO, *K2tog, YO, K3, YO, K2, (ssk) 3 times, YO, ssk, YO, K1, YO, sl 1-K2tog-psso, YO, K1, YO; rep from *, end last rep K2tog, YO, K3, YO, K2, (ssk) 3 times, YO, ssk, YO, K2.

Row 39: K2, YO, *K2tog, YO, K2tog, K2, YO, K1, YO, (sl 1-K2tog-psso) twice, ssk, YO, K1, YO, sl 1-K2tog-psso, YO, K1, YO; rep from *, end last rep K2tog, YO, K2tog, K2, YO, K1, YO, (sl 1-K2tog-psso) twice, ssk, YO, K2.

Row 40 (WS): P4, *P2tog-tbl, P16; rep from *, end last rep P2tog-tbl, P11.

Row 41: K2, YO, *K2tog, YO, K2tog, K2, YO, K3, YO, sl 1-K2tog-psso, YO, K1, YO, sl 1-K2tog-psso, YO, K1, YO; rep from *, end last rep K2tog, YO, K2tog, K2, YO, K3, YO, sl 1-K2tog-psso, YO, K2.

Row 43: K2, YO, *K2tog, YO, (K2tog, K2, YO) twice, K1, YO, ssk, YO, K1, YO, sl 1-K2tog-psso, YO, K1, YO; rep from *, end last rep K2tog, YO, (K2tog, K2, YO) twice, K1, YO, ssk, YO, K2.

Row 44 (WS): Purl.

Rep rows 29–44 twice more.

BOTTOM EDGE

Next row (RS): K3, *K2tog, YO, K1; rep from *, end K2.

Next row (WS): Purl.

BO loosely, using size 13 needle. Weave in tails and block.

Chart A Yoke
Starts on row 17 (RS).

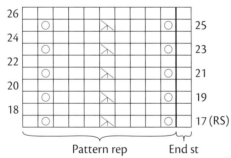

Key

☐	K on RS, P on WS	◪	P2tog
▨	No stitch	◩	P2tog-tbl
⊙	YO	⊠	sl 1-K2tog-psso
◹	ssk	◿	K3tog
◺	K2tog		

Chart B Body
Starts on row 29 (RS).

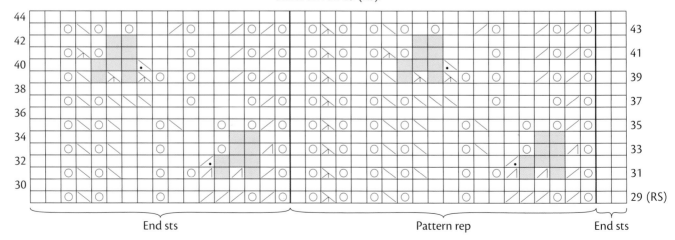

Bigfoot Story

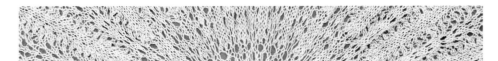

$\mathcal{W}$E WERE REMODELING, and I had a sense of exactly what I wanted my front entryway to look like. But I had no idea if the tile I wanted even existed.

A friend suggested a store in Redwood City, and I headed there to check it out. It turned out the place was going out of business. Clearly this was the time to buy. I looked around, and there were my tiles! The perfect shade of heathered peach in just the right size.

It was a stormy day, and as the owner was putting the tiles in my car for me, I noticed there were only six boxes. "Hey," I said, "I bought seven."

"Oh, don't worry," he told me, "six'll do that square footage just fine. I only charged you for six anyway." He clearly wanted to be done and back inside before he got too soaked.

I protested, he held firm, and I let it go, defeated. I have memories of my mother running out of red wool just before she finished a sweater she'd been working on for months. Never underbuy on materials.

Then came the day, weeks later, when I arrived home to find my guy laying those tiles, pointing, "Look. Almost every one in this box was broken. If, and only if, there is not a single broken one in that last box, I will have enough." If not . . .

I tore out of there. The whole way up the freeway, I was scolding myself, thinking, "You knew, you knew! How much is it going to cost to pay Henry to rip out all his hard work and start over with something I don't like as much?"

The store was still open and they still had some. I couldn't believe it. The owner apologized, and I went racing home. I walked in just as Henry was placing the final tile in the back corner. He'd done it. Every tile in that last box had been whole after all.

One recent Saturday, I bought two skeins of Frog Tree alpaca yarn for a quick scarf. I launched into this shawl instead, because that's simply what it wanted to be. I knitted away, not knowing if I would be able to finish, if maybe the rest of the dye lot had sold out. Tuesday, just after the shop opened, I flung open the shop door and yelled, "Nobody touch that alpaca! It's mine!"

Kat, a staffer, cracked up. I bought two more skeins from her and used just one of them. The shawl is quite short, I decided later. It's good to know I have that extra skein; if it bugs me, I can always undo the cast off and add to the length.

Sometimes being stingy on supplies gets you enough. But, man, does it feel a whole lot better to have a backup supply, just in case.

Bigfoot Shawl

I called my smaller Feather and Fan variant that uses rows
14 and 16 of this pattern "Rabbit Tracks" on my Web site.
This shawl begins with that pattern. When I doodled and came up
with a pattern that had double the number of stitches,
"Bigfoot" seemed just the right name.

Materials

- 3 skeins of fingering-weight Alpaca from Frog Tree Yarns (100% alpaca; 215 yds; 50 g per skein) in color 005 Tan (**1**)
- Size 8 (5 mm) circular needle, 32" to 40" long, or size to obtain gauge
- Size 11 (8 mm) needle for binding off
- Tapestry needle for weaving in tails

Skill Level

■■□□

Easy

Finished Blocked Measurements

Length: Approx 16"
Bottom Circumference: Approx 120"

Gauge

16-st rep = 5" over body pattern (chart B or rows 28–31), blocked

Instructions

CO 12 sts loosely, doubling yarn for the CO row and keeping sts at least 1" apart (see "Neck Edges" on page 10).

Row 1 (and all WS rows): Purl.

Row 2 (RS): (YO, K1) across—24 sts.

Row 4: (YO, K1) across—48 sts.

Row 6: (YO, K1) across—96 sts.

Row 8: K2, *K2tog, YO, K1; rep from *, end K1.

Row 10: K2, *YO, K1, K2tog; rep from *, end K1.

Row 12: (YO, K1) across—192 sts.

Row 13: Purl across, working 2 sts into last YO (the YO made at the beginning of the previous row)—193 sts.

YOKE

Worked over a multiple of 8 + 1 sts. St count varies from row to row. See chart A on page 36 for rows 14–17 if you prefer to work from charts.

Row 14 (RS): *K1, ssk, (YO, K1) 3 times, YO, K2tog; rep from *, end K1.

Row 15 (WS): Purl.

Row 16: *K1, ssk, K5, K2tog, rep from *, end K1.

Row 17 (WS): Purl.

Rows 18–25: Rep rows 14–17 twice more.

Row 26: (K1, YO) across, end K1—385 sts.

Row 27 (WS): Purl.

BODY

Worked over a multiple of 16 + 1 sts. St count varies from row to row. See chart B on page 36 for rows 28–31 if you prefer to work from charts.

Row 28 (RS): *K1, (ssk) twice, (YO, K1) 7 times, YO, (K2tog) twice; rep from *, end K1.

Row 29 (WS): Purl.

Row 30: *K1, (ssk) twice, K11, (K2tog) twice; rep from *, end K1.

Row 31 (WS): Purl.

Rep rows 28–31 until shawl is 16" or desired length.

BOTTOM EDGE

BO loosely, using size 11 needle.

BIGFOOT SHAWL (larger version)

Alternatively, for a very generously sized shawl, I used Lisa Souza's Kid Mohair yarn, one 1,000-yard skein in the Shade Garden colorway, and knitted it densely and warmly on size 9 needles.

Chart A Yoke
Starts on row 14 (RS).

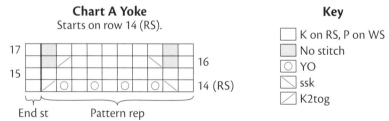

End st   Pattern rep

Key

☐	K on RS, P on WS
▨	No stitch
⊙	YO
◺	ssk
◿	K2tog

Chart B Body
Starts on row 28 (RS).

End st   Pattern rep

Julia's Story

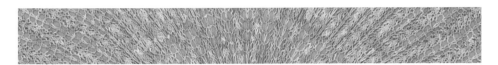

I WROTE THIS *when it happened and shared it with Julia, Camille's mom.*

Yesterday after church, people were visiting a bit. I noticed Brandon, age four, had scrambled to the top of three stacking chairs, and another dad was smiling and talking to him. Brandon, being good, was sitting on his throne rather than standing and playing king of the mountain. His sister Camille, almost two, had followed him and was sitting on top of a two-chair-high stack next to him.

She'd been there awhile. Brandon scrambled off to something else. Camille wasn't looking too sure of herself, so I went over and played peek-a-boo, to her great delight. But every time I stopped, her face got closer to crying.

Suddenly I got it. She wasn't very high up at all, but I looked at her and asked, "Do you want to get down?"

"Yes!" she wailed. Just like all babies who can climb up stairs long before they can climb down them, she was stuck. And scared. And suddenly very alone, with her hero big brother gone.

I scooped her up. Rather than squirming down and running to her daddy, this quite shy little girl threw her arms around my neck and held on tight for dear life. She was clinging as if to say, "Hold me! Don't leave me!"

I had almost forgotten what it feels like to be so needed by a small child. My youngest is a teenager big enough to put *me* in the grocery cart. I hugged her back, sweet child, realizing that actually, she was a fair bit higher up than she'd been just a second ago. But what a difference.

I savored it briefly as I walked over to her dad, praying for my balance to hold. With my cane dangling from my elbow as I held Camille in both arms, with both of hers around my neck, I needed help, too. The last thing that child needed was for the adult she trusted to stumble. I felt the floor carefully with my feet, because muscle feedback is the only way I can maintain my balance. But somehow, Camille's weight gave me some of that feedback, too. I found myself walking to her daddy as gracefully as if there were no problem. She had helped me as much as I had helped her.

Camille's mother, Julia, is my dear friend, so I made this shawl for her. What Camille gets is a little moment in her life written down, one that speaks of so many others that will all add up over time. Through teenagerhood and beyond, she can be comforted by knowing how many loving arms there have been and always will be, ready to lift her up. And for her to lift up, too.

Julia's Shawl

This was designed in response to someone's telling me that lace was too complex for her to attempt. Note that with a pattern that is only six stitches long, this is very much the simplest shawl in the book and a good one to use as the background to show off the effects of a hand-painted yarn; the visual effects of hand paints tend to obscure any more elaborate stitch pattern anyway.

Materials

- ۞ 1 skein, but without a yard to spare, of Petal from Lisa Souza Knitwear and Dyeworks (50% silk, 50% merino; 667 yds; ⅓ lb per skein) in color Tropical Pink **1**
- ۞ Size 9 (5.5 mm) circular needle, 32" to 40" long, or size to obtain gauge
- ۞ Size 13 (9 mm) knitting needle for binding off
- ۞ Tapestry needle for weaving in tails

Skill Level

■☐☐☐
Beginner

Finished Blocked Measurements

Length: Approx 18"
Bottom Circumference: Approx 128"

Gauge

6-st rep = 2" over pattern st (chart or rows 9 and 10), blocked

Instructions

CO 7 sts loosely, doubling yarn for the CO row and keeping sts at least 1" apart (see "Neck Edges" on page 10). For a wider neck, CO 13 and begin knitting with row 3.

Row 1 (RS): (K1, YO) across, end K1—13 sts.

Row 2 (and all WS rows): Purl.

Row 3: (K1, YO) across, end K1—25 sts.

Row 5: (K1, YO) across, end K1—49 sts.

Row 7: (K1, YO) across, end K1—97 sts.

Row 8: Purl.

YOKE

Worked over a multiple of 6 + 1 sts. See chart on page 40 for rows 9–12 if you prefer to work from charts.

Rows 9 and 11 (RS): K1, *YO, K1, sl 1-K2tog-psso, K1, YO, K1, rep from *.

Rows 10 and 12 (WS): Purl.

Row 13: (K1, YO) across, end K1—193 sts.

Row 14: Purl.

Rows 15–28: Rep rows 9 and 10 seven more times.

Row 29: (K1, YO) across, end K1—385 sts.

Row 30 (WS): Purl.

BODY

Cont to rep rows 9 and 10 until shawl measures 18" or desired length.

Note: When going from the yoke to the body, doubling the number of stitches, the pattern is offset halfway from the previous segment like the three endpoints of a Y, but the single knit stitch that runs between the decreases continues in an unbroken line all the way down.

BOTTOM EDGE

BO loosely, using size 13 needle. Weave in tails and block.

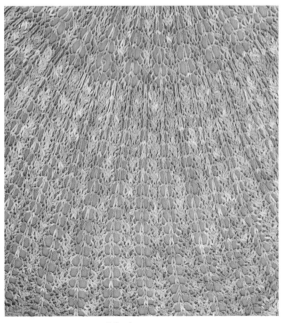

Stitch pattern

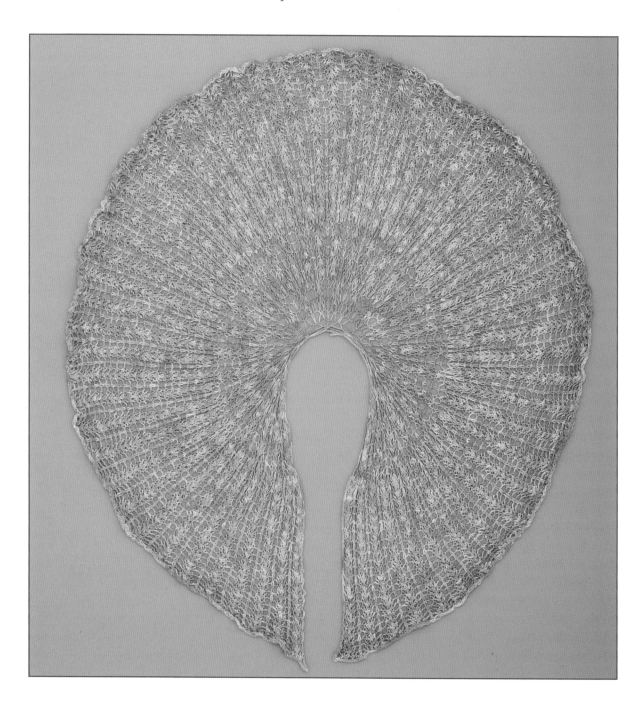

Shawl Chart
Starts on row 9 (RS).

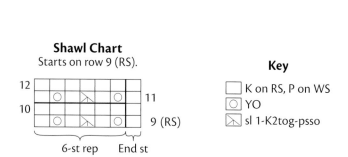

Key

☐ K on RS, P on WS
◌ YO
⧄ sl 1-K2tog-psso

JULIA'S SHAWL (faster version)

For a faster version of Julia's Shawl that is 24" long, I used one 1,000-yard skein of Kid Mohair yarn from Lisa Souza Dyeworks in the colorway Pacific. The single skein was enough to make two shawls. Here's the pattern for this version.

Needles: Sizes 10 and 11—I used the 10s only for doing the increase rows 2, 4, 6, and 8, to keep the yarn overs to a reasonable size, but you could certainly use just the 11s throughout.

Gauge: One 6-st rep = 3" over pattern rows 10–15 or Julia chart on page 40

Using size 11s, CO 9 sts very loosely.

Row 1 (and all WS rows): Purl.

Row 2 (RS): (K1, YO) across, end K2—16 sts.

Row 4: (K1, YO) across, end K1—31 sts.

Row 6: (K1, YO) across, end K1—61 sts.

Row 8: (K1, YO) across, end K1—121 sts.

Rows 10, 12, and 14: K1, *YO, K1, sl 1-K2tog-psso, K1, YO, K1; rep from *.

Rows 11, 13, and 15: Purl.

Row 16: (K1, YO) across, end K1—241 sts.

Row 17: Purl.

Rep rows 10 and 11 above (or see rows 9 and 10 of Julia chart on page 40) 19 times or until desired length, to keep it simple like the original, or as I did with this one, follow the instructions for rows 22–30 of Constance's Shawl (page 47) as an added edging.

Monterey Story

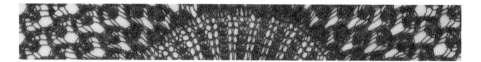

I FELL IN LOVE with penguins after one at the Monterey Bay Aquarium spent five minutes (till my family pulled me away) mimicking me, following me, playing with me from its side of the glass, ignoring everybody else who was trying to get its attention. It was my penguin, or I was its human just then, take your pick. A few times, it seemed like all that accumulating joy just exploded into penguin energy, and it dove across its pool to work it off, coming straight back to me afterward. Those birds swim fast! And when I laughed at that, it threw its head back and waggled its open beak to look like a laugh, too. It was like playing with an absolutely devoted two-year-old. Penguins are so cool.

Now, how would you knit a penguin motif into a lace shawl? There were other things to enjoy at the aquarium, even if they didn't follow me around and adore me. Easier things, should I admit, to figure out how to knit. And so I came up with a design depicting water bubbles at the top of the ocean's surface, up around the neck, with a kelp forest just below, swaying gently back and forth in the rhythm of the tide, the rhythm of the needles working the rows. Further down, I envisioned a school of jellyfish in the more naturally deep blue-green of the ocean, rather than the ultraviolet blue water with the jellies lit up vivid orange the way they show them in the aquarium display. Visiting Monterey may be as close to scuba diving and enjoying the life within the ocean as I'll ever get, and I wanted to somehow take it all home and keep it with me.

One of these days, one way or another, I think I'm going to have to knit me some kind of a penguin.

Monterey Shawl

I knitted this shawl for my friend Michelle Romero, a dedicated marine biology enthusiast. The "jellyfish" in rows 30–37 are Barbara Walker's Shower Stitch, knitted from the top down for an entirely different effect.

Materials

- ⑥ 5 skeins of 100% Alpaca from Pacific Meadows Alpaca (150 yds per skein) in color Light Blue [③]
- ⑥ Size 9 (5.5 mm) circular needle, 32" to 40" long, or size to obtain gauge
- ⑥ Size 13 (9 mm) knitting needle for binding off
- ⑥ Tapestry needle for weaving in tails

Note: I bought a 1,800-yd/450-g cone, made my own hank, and washed the yarn. I used 5 oz for this shawl.

Skill Level

■■■▶
Experienced

Finished Blocked Measurements

Length: Approx 19"
Bottom Circumference: Approx 127"

Gauge

12-st rep = 4¼" over body pattern (chart B or rows 30–37), blocked

Instructions

CO 12 sts loosely, doubling yarn for the CO row and keeping sts at least 1" apart (see "Neck Edges" on page 10).

Row 1 (and all WS rows through row 29): Purl.

Row 2 (RS): (K1, YO) across, end K1—23 sts.

Row 4: (K1, YO) across, end K1—45 sts.

Row 6: K2, *K2tog, YO, K1; rep from *, end K1.

Row 8: (YO, K1) across—90 sts.

Row 10: Rep row 6.

Row 12: K2, *YO, K1, K2tog; rep from *, end K1.

Row 14: Rep row 6.

Row 16: You need to inc from 90 to 181 sts, so, you must work 1 extra st besides doing (YO, K1) across. I did it this way: YO, (K1, YO) twice, pick up the bar below the next st and knit into that, (K1, YO) across, end K1. But it doesn't really matter how you choose to inc 1 extra st.

YOKE

Worked over a multiple of 6 + 1 sts. See chart A on page 45 for rows 18–27 if you prefer to work from charts. Cont to purl WS rows.

Row 18 (RS): K1, *YO, K1, sl 1-K2tog-psso, K1, YO, K1; rep from *.

Row 19: Purl.

Rows 20–27: Repeat rows 18 and 19.

Row 28: You need to increase from 181 to 364 sts, so you need 2 additional sts beyond doubling the number of sts. I worked the inc as follows: YO, (K1, YO) 3 times, pick up the bar below the next st and knit into that, knit next st, *YO, K1, rep from * to last 3 sts, pick up the bar below the next st and knit into that, knit next st, (YO, K1) twice—364 sts.

Row 29 (WS): Purl.

BODY

Worked over a multiple of 12 + 4 sts. See chart B on page 45 for rows 30–37 if you prefer to work from charts.

Row 30 (RS): K2, *K2tog, YO, K2, K2tog, (YO) twice, ssk, K2, YO, ssk; rep from *, end K2.

Row 31 (WS): P2, *P3, P2tog-tbl, YO, (K1, P1) into the 2 YOs of previous row, YO, P2tog, P3; rep from *, end P2.

Row 32: K2, *K2, K2tog, YO, K4, YO, ssk, K2; rep from *, end K2.

Row 33: P2, *P3tog-tbl, YO, P1, YO, P4, YO, P1, YO, P3tog; rep from *, end P2.

Row 34: K2, *YO, ssk, K2, YO, ssk, K2tog, YO, K2, K2tog, YO; rep from *, end K2, noting that the YOs combined at the beginning and ending of rep form a double YO.

Row 35: P2, *P1, YO, P2tog, P6, P2tog-tbl, YO, K1; rep from *, ending P2. Note that the P1 at the beg and the K1 at the end of rep form a K1, P1 into the double YOs of row 34.

Row 36: K2, *K2, YO, ssk, K4, K2tog, YO, K2; rep from *, end K2.

Row 37: P2, *P2, YO, P1, YO, P3tog, P3tog-tbl, YO, P1, YO, P2; rep from *, end P2.

Rep rows 30–37 a total of 5 times or longer as desired.

BOTTOM EDGE

Next RS row: Rep row 6.

BO, using size 13 needle as you purl back. This gives you a better bottom edge than straight binding off from the last row. Weave in tails and block.

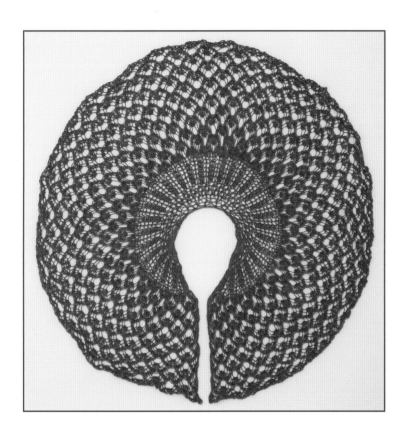

Chart A Yoke
Starts on row 18 (RS).

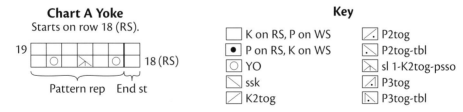

Pattern rep | End st

Key

☐	K on RS, P on WS	◪	P2tog
●	P on RS, K on WS	◩	P2tog-tbl
◯	YO	⬕	sl 1-K2tog-psso
◻	ssk	◪	P3tog
◿	K2tog	◺	P3tog-tbl

Chart B Body
Starts on row 30 (RS).

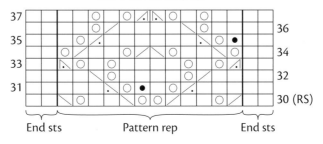

End sts | Pattern rep | End sts

Constance's Story

CONSTANCE WAS a member of my knitting group, and it was hard not to feel like I was reluctantly kicking her out. I was over at her house helping her get it ready for sale. She was moving from San Jose to the Gold Country—a place in the mountains—after having lived in the Bay Area of northern California all her life. In Constance's house, children's books were in order on a bookcase, placed just so, to look pretty. That wouldn't have lasted long if they'd been around my kids!

I envied her. She had, ahead of her, acres to look at from the top of a wide hill, eagles soaring, wild turkeys gobbling, foxes hunting, the occasional bear or mountain lion to look out for. Room for horses and for every flower she could possibly think of in a large garden—a space and place as serene as knitting for a friend.

Over the years since then, Constance has come back to town to visit relatives at Thanksgiving, or to head over to Stitches West nearby, the gathering for all things knitting on the West Coast. So, in addition to our streams of emails, we still get to see each other occasionally. It's about a three-hour drive. She came to my house once with a wool sweater, which we overdyed together. Then I, wanting to see how it fit once it had cooled outside of the dye bath, and hoping it hadn't shrunk too much, tried it on, wet and all. Tiny twirls of teal went flinging across my white wall, creating the Constance Harker Sweater Memorial (till my husband painted it over.)

One day, soon after she'd moved, Constance wrote to say she'd looked out the windows, distressed that a fox must have gotten at the chickens. There were feathers flying everywhere, but so evenly, floating down. . .

And her daughter yelled, "Mom, look! It's snowing!" And she typed to me, sheepishly, "Um. Yeah. I knew that."

I laughed and described having had to shovel more than my height's worth of snow during seventeen days in March, just before moving to California, where things were already green and blooming. Paradise!

I had to knit Constance a shawl. Throw a chicken ball and have some snow soup. Birds of a feather knit together no matter the distance. Hey, old friend, this one's for you.

Constance's Shawl

Barbara Walker's Smiling Diamonds, knit from the top down, reminds me of the spots at the top of a young golden eagle's wings, and the solid half diamond helps shape the bottom of the wings. I love how the colors came out like a scattered-clouds day for the eagle to fly in!

Materials

- ᪥ 2 skeins of Sock! Merino from Lisa Souza Knitwear and Dyeworks (100% superfine merino; 560 yds; 4 oz per skein) in color Blue Sky 【2】
- ᪥ Size 9 (5.5 mm) circular needle, 32" to 40" long, or size to obtain gauge
- ᪥ Size 13 (9 mm) knitting needle for binding off
- ᪥ Tapestry needle for weaving in tails

Skill Level

■■□□

Easy

Finished Blocked Measurements

Length: Approx 20"
Bottom Circumference: Approx 99"

Gauge

12-st rep = 4⅛" over body pattern (chart C or rows 22–41), blocked

Instructions

CO 19 sts loosely, doubling yarn for the CO row and keeping sts at least 1" apart (see "Neck Edges" on page 10).

Row 1 (and all WS rows): Purl.
Row 2 (RS): (K1, YO) across, end K1—37 sts.
Row 4: (K1, YO) across, end K1—73 sts.
Row 5: Purl.

YOKE

Worked over a multiple of 6 + 1 sts. Cont to purl WS rows.

Yoke Pattern 1

See chart A on page 49 for rows 6–9 if you prefer to work from charts.

Row 6 (RS): K1, *YO, ssk, K1, K2tog, YO, K1; rep from *.

Row 8: K1, *YO, K1, sl 1-K2tog-psso, K1, YO, K1; rep from *.

Row 9 (WS): Purl.

Row 10: (K1, YO) across, end K1—145 sts.

Rows 12–15: Rep rows 6–9 once more.

Yoke Pattern 2

See chart B on page 49 for rows 16–19 if you prefer to work from charts.

Row 16 (RS): K1, *K2tog, YO, K1, YO, ssk, K1; rep from *.

Row 18: K2tog, *(K1, YO) twice, K1, sl 1-K2tog-psso, rep from *, end ssk.

Row 20: (K1, YO) across, end K1—289 sts.

Row 21 (WS): Purl.

BODY

Worked over a multiple of 12 + 1 sts. See chart C on page 49 for rows 22–41 if you prefer to work from charts. Cont to purl WS rows.

Row 22 (RS): K1, *YO, ssk, K7, K2tog, YO, K1; rep from *.

Row 24: K1, *K1, YO, ssk, K5, K2tog, YO, K2; rep from *.

Row 26: K1, *(YO, ssk) twice, K3, (K2tog, YO) twice, K1; rep from *.

Row 28: K1, *K1, (YO, ssk) twice, K1, (K2tog, YO) twice, K2; rep from *.

Row 30: K1, *(YO, ssk) twice, YO, sl 1-K2tog-psso, YO, (K2tog, YO) twice, K1; rep from *.

Row 32: K1, *K3, K2tog, YO, K1, YO, ssk, K4; rep from *.

Row 34: K1, *K2, K2tog, YO, K3, YO, ssk, K3; rep from *.

Row 36: K1, *K1, (K2tog, YO) twice, K1 (YO, ssk) twice, K2; rep from *.

Row 38: K1, *(K2tog, YO) twice, K3, (YO, ssk) twice, K1; rep from *.

Row 40: K2tog, YO, *(K2tog, YO) twice, K1, (YO, ssk) twice, YO, sl 1-K2tog-psso, YO; rep from *, end last rep (YO, ssk) 3 times.

Row 41 (WS): Purl.

Rep rows 22–41 until shawl measures 20" or desired length.

BOTTOM EDGING

BO loosely, using size 13 needle. Weave in tails and block.

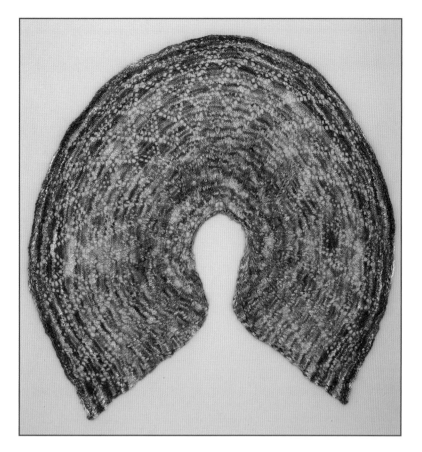

Chart A Yoke Pattern 1
Starts on row 6 (RS).

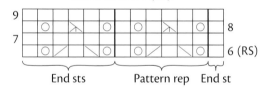

End sts   Pattern rep   End st

Chart B Yoke Pattern 2
Starts on row 16 (RS).

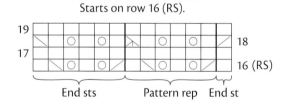

End sts   Pattern rep   End st

Chart C Body
Starts on row 22 (RS).

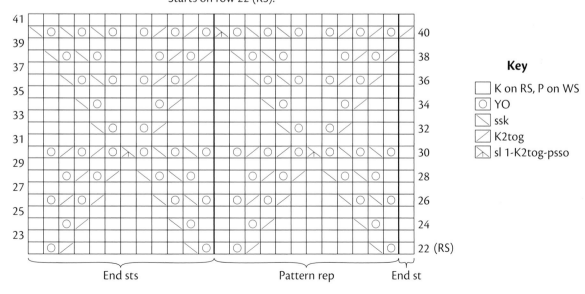

End sts   Pattern rep   End st

Key

☐ K on RS, P on WS
◯ YO
◺ ssk
◿ K2tog
⧖ sl 1-K2tog-psso

Blue Jay Story

ON A CHILLY SPRING morning, I looked out my window as a sparrow landed on a downspout. It slid down the slippery metal, fluttered its wings, held its place a moment, slid, and fluttered again and again, finally landing against the wall with the gentlest thud. I watched it and thought, "Yeah, bird, I've had days like that."

Soon a dove's nest was in my backyard. Hatchlings! I set four ounces of green cashmere outside to dry, and glanced over later to see the skein hitting the patio and a jay flying off.

Which should certainly have warned me. Not long after, I was pulling a pound of alpaca out of the dye pot, a perfect denim blue. Yes! I wanted to knit it immediately. I could hog-tie the hank to my antenna and hit the freeway. (Why am I suddenly reminded of the BMW photo with the license plate BLOND upside down?) Or I could hang it outside in the sun. I'd be knitting by evening.

I think I earned that license plate. I picked up my hank and went, "WHAT?" Oh goodness. I ran to the hot water and poured in liquid detergent. It was too late. Nesting season. My yarn had been targeted by bird poop. Man, that bird had been eating a lot lately. And man, did it bleach out my yarn where it hit.

Scream, laugh, cry, all at once. "I'm not guano wear it, you wear it!"

I cleaned it off, got my dye back out, and tried to fix it. I threw it back in the dye pot. I let it dry in its own sweet time over the bathtub, thinking "Let's keep that door shut. I don't even want to have to see it when I walk down the hall." And then I threw the dry yarn in the back of the closet, knowing it had been so exactly the color I'd wanted before the bird had gotten to it.

Eventually I got frustrated enough to grab the yarn and think, "I still like that color," and I launched into this shawl, having no idea how the variations would play out. It wanted to be a blue jay shawl. It was a blue jay color. It was going to be a blue jay shawl. The bird had claimed it. It beats calling it the bird-poop shawl.

So no. I have no idea how to reproduce these lovely variations. I guess you'd have to start with what the bird had been eating? Beats me.

Recently, a woman in an elevator, just before the ride upward ended in a gentle thud at our feet, tried vainly to buy the shawl off my back, even after I tried to put her off ruefully, laughingly telling her the story. She completely made my day.

Blue Jay Shawl

Barbara Walker's Checkerboard Mesh always reminds me of playing chalk-on-the-driveway hopscotch as a kid.

Materials

- ⑥ 5 skeins of 100% Alpaca from Pacific Meadows Alpaca (150 yds per skein) in color Light Blue with added Jacquard acid dye in Navy ⓵⓷
- ⑥ Size 9 (5.5 mm) circular needle, 32" to 40" long, or size to obtain gauge
- ⑥ Size 13 (9 mm) knitting needle for binding off
- ⑥ Tapestry needle for weaving in tails

Note: *I bought a 1,800-yd/450-g cone, made my own hanks, and washed the yarn. I used just over 6 oz for this shawl. The yarn was overdyed with the help of a blue jay.*

Skill Level

◼◼◼☐

Intermediate

Finished Blocked Measurements

Length: Approx 19"

Bottom Circumference: Approx 142½"

Gauge

10-st rep = 3¾" over body pattern (chart B or rows 22–41), blocked

Instructions

CO 12 sts loosely, keeping sts at least 1" apart (see "Neck Edges" on page 10).

Row 1 (and all WS rows): Purl.

Row 2 (RS): (YO, K1) across—24 sts.

Row 4: (YO, K1) across—48 sts.

Row 6: (YO, K1) across—96 sts.

Row 8: Knit.

Row 10: (K1, YO) across, end K1—191 sts.

Row 11 (WS): Purl.

YOKE

Worked over a multiple of 10 + 1 sts. See chart A on page 53 for rows 12–19 if you prefer to work from charts. Cont to purl WS rows.

Rows 12 and 14 (RS): K1, *YO, K3, sl 1-K2tog-psso, K3, YO, K1; rep from *.

Rows 16 and 18: K2tog, *K3, YO, K1, YO, K3, sl 1-K2tog-psso; rep from *, end last rep with ssk instead of sl 1-K2tog-psso.

Row 20: (YO, K1) across, knitting twice into last st—383 sts.

Row 21: Purl twice into last st—384 sts.

Yoke pattern. Note that I did not use a double strand of yarn for the cast on.

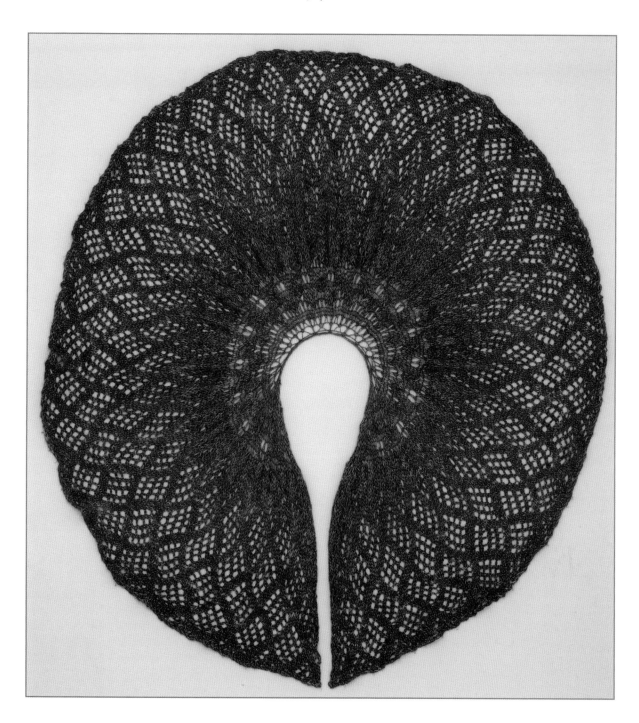

Chart A Yoke
Starts on row 12 (RS).

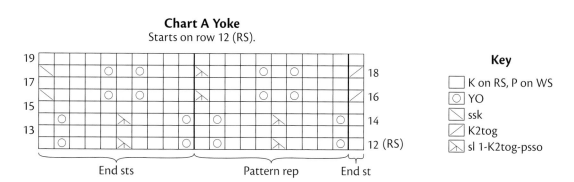

End sts   Pattern rep   End st

Key

☐ K on RS, P on WS
◯ YO
◻ ssk
◻ K2tog
◻ sl 1-K2tog-psso

BODY

Worked over a multiple of 10 + 4 sts. See chart B below for rows 22–41 if you prefer to work from charts. Cont to purl WS rows.

Row 22 (RS): K4, *YO, ssk, K1, (K2tog, YO) twice, K3; rep from *.

Row 24: *K3, (YO, ssk) twice, K1, K2tog, YO; rep from *, end K4.

Row 26: K2, *(YO, ssk) 3 times, K4; rep from *, end YO, ssk.

Row 28: K1, *(YO, ssk) 4 times, K2; rep from *, end YO, ssk, K1.

Row 30: Rep row 26.

Row 32: Rep row 24.

Row 34: Rep row 22.

Row 36: K2tog, YO, *K4, (K2tog, YO) 3 times; rep from *, end K2.

Row 38: K1, K2tog, YO, *K2, (K2tog, YO) 4 times; rep from *, end K1.

Row 40: Rep row 36.

Row 41 (WS): Purl.

Rep rows 22–41 twice more.

BOTTOM EDGE

BO very loosely, using size 13 needle. Weave in tails and block.

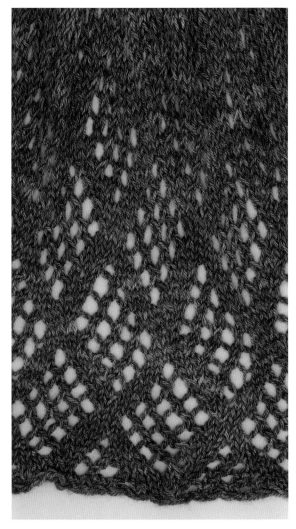

Body pattern

Chart B Body
Starts on row 22 (RS).

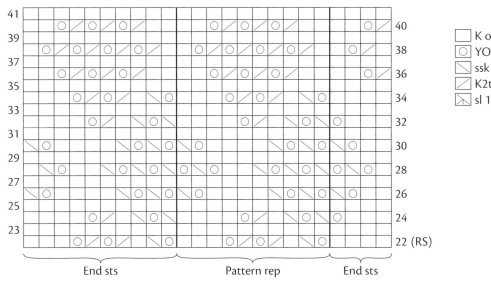

Key

☐	K on RS, P on WS
⊡	YO
◺	ssk
◹	K2tog
◩	sl 1-K2tog-psso

End sts   Pattern rep   End sts

Carlsbad Story

LISA SOUZA'S hand-painted colorway Sky Drama reminds me of the summer of '69 when, like so many other families during the Vietnam era, we hit the highway with a camper to see for ourselves what America really was. I was 10.

Mom soon decided I needed to knit so that I'd stop bugging my little sister in the back seat. I stood in a store in some random town and picked out an acrylic yarn in red, purple, blue, green, and orange. Recently, Lisa's hand-dyed yarn reminded me of that trip as I found myself again reaching for a skein in a mixture of colors, a sunset swirling in soft silk.

At Carlsbad Caverns in New Mexico, the rangers announced they would turn out all the lights just so we could see, for the first time in our lives, what true darkness was.

In anticipation, I sat down on the trail, and someone's small child climbed in my lap. When the lights went off, I could not have told she was there unless she shifted her weight or spoke. And spoke we did! We both exclaimed, "Are you there?" The utter absence of color and light was an experience I'll never forget, and I wondered if this was what it would be like if I were ever to go blind. Having for a few weeks lost a portion of my sight this past July, I am grateful for hands that can feel wool wrapping around wood. It wasn't a blackness. It was an absence of the left page while reading the right, a constant distraction of, "Is it there?" Maybe choosing that yarn from Lisa was more of a declaration than I'd realized of how very good it is to be able to fully experience its colors.

As that day turned to evening, we gathered on rows of wooden benches set up before the mouth of the caverns. There was a large population of bats just inside, and we were told they came flying out at sunset to eat the mosquitoes, not to bite us. Bats were our friends. I was trying earnestly not to be dubious: but do they poop in flight? I mean, there were so many!

There was a beautiful sunset to watch and crickets in concert, but sunsets go in awfully slow motion. The ranger told bat stories as we waited. A year earlier, they'd had a woman there with a beehive hairdo. He held his hands high above his head, describing her hair. "Well," he said, "it seems there was this one baby bat, and it got tired fast. It just couldn't quite keep enough lift under its wings." For one stylish woman out there somewhere, there was definitely some "Sky Drama" that night.

Carlsbad Scarf

*Silk drapes beautifully, and this scarf will not maintain
a starched-crisp width like a blocked wool yarn would.*

Materials

- ᪥ 1 skein of Glacier Silk Yarn from Lisa Souza Knitwear and Dyeworks (100% Bombyx cultivated silk; 273 yds; 3.5 oz per skein) in color Sky Drama (**4**)
- ᪥ Size 10½ (6.5 mm) needles or size to obtain gauge
- ᪥ Tapestry needle for weaving in tails

Skill Level

■☐☐☐
Beginner

Finished Blocked Measurements

Width: 8½"
Length: 55"
Note: Add multiples of 10 to knit a wider scarf.

Gauge

33 sts = 8" over body pattern (chart or rows 1–12), blocked

Instructions

CO 33 sts.

See chart below for rows 1–12 if you prefer working from charts.

Row 1 (and all WS rows): Purl.

Rows 2, 4, and 6 (RS): K1, K2tog, *K3, YO, K1, YO, K3, sl 1-K2tog-psso; rep from * to last 3 sts, end last rep ssk, K1.

Rows 8, 10, and 12: K2, *YO, K3, sl 1-K2tog-psso, K3, YO, K1; rep from *, end YO, K2.

Rep rows 1–12 until scarf is 55" or desired length.

BO all sts. Weave in tails and block.

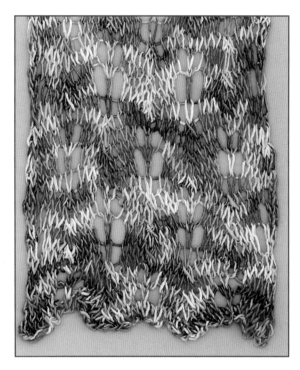

Pattern stitch

Scarf Chart
Starts on row 1 (WS).

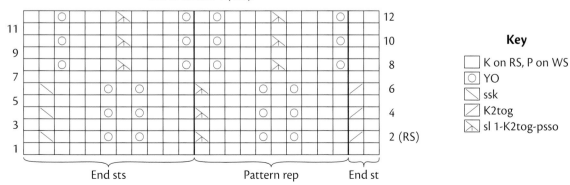

Key

☐ K on RS, P on WS
○ YO
◹ ssk
◿ K2tog
⧖ sl 1-K2tog-psso

Tara's Story

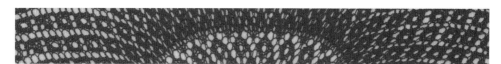

*T*HIS PATTERN came to be because I liked the yarn. I liked the stitch pattern. But I don't know yet whom it's for.

Sometimes knitting is like that. Something just leaps onto the needles and demands to be, right now! And you have to wait for it to tell you why. Like Tara's afghan, which I'd made in two strands of kid mohair in light pink. Just because.

Seven years earlier I'd been diagnosed with lupus, and my arthritis was severe at first. I was advised to swim at an indoor pool. But there was no way I could afford a babysitter. How on earth was I going to do this?

My friend Lisa took a deep breath, wondering what she was letting herself in for, and volunteered to watch my preschoolers while I swam if I would then watch her son David while she worked out—every weekday for the foreseeable future. Understand that if she'd wanted to go running, all she'd have had to do was put her toddler in a stroller and go. She was offering a gift of her hours and days I could never repay, a gift that did much to ease the burden of my drastically changed life.

We did that for three years, as Lisa had two more children and mine grew older. I expected to keep watching hers, but it was not to be. They moved to Michigan, but at least their grandma lived near me, an excuse to come visit.

But Grandma had had cancer, and it came back. I attended her funeral. Two days later, Lisa and her children came over before heading back to the airport. My children were on spring break, and we were having a grand time getting reacquainted. My older son, Richard, a teenage beanpole, swung the smaller children around and around till they fell down laughing.

Suddenly seven-year-old Tara crumpled into tears. Grandma was gone! Why was everybody being so happy when Grandma was gone? Didn't they know?

And just then she saw that half-forgotten pink mohair afghan in the corner. She ran to it. And immediately I knew why I had made it.

I scooped her up with the afghan. I told her how I'd made it and almost given it away, but it just hadn't felt right. Now I knew. Now I knew. A pink fluffy afghan from California for a little girl to hold tight, to feel Grandma was smiling over her.

I don't know whom this shawl is for yet. I've tried to get it to tell me for months. It's not quite Lisa's color. But when the time comes, I will know exactly who it was for all along. Tara taught me that.

Tara's Redwood Burl Shawl

Barbara Walker's Pierced Diamond pattern gives
a marvelous swoop to this shawl.

Materials

- ⚘ 9 balls of Baby Cashmere from Peruvian Collection (60% baby alpaca, 30% merino, 10% cashmere; 25 g; 100 m/109 yds per ball) in color 1960 ⑴
- ⚘ Size 9 (5.5 mm) circular needle, 32" to 40" long, or size to obtain gauge
- ⚘ Size 13 (9 mm) knitting needle for binding off
- ⚘ Tapestry needle for weaving in tails

Skill Level

◼◼◼▢
Intermediate

Finished Blocked Measurements

Length: Approx 22"
Bottom Circumference: Approx 141"

Gauge

6-st rep = 2⅓" over body pattern (chart or rows 14–25), blocked

Instructions

CO 24 sts loosely, doubling yarn for the CO row and keeping sts at least 1" apart (see "Neck Edges" on page 10).

Row 1 (and all WS rows): Purl.

Row 2 (RS): (K1, YO) across, end K1—47 sts.

Row 4: Knit.

Row 6: (K1, YO) across, end K1—93 sts.

Row 8: K2, *K2tog, YO, K1; rep from *, end K1.

Row 10: K2, *YO, K1, K2tog; rep from *, end K1.

Row 12: K2, (YO, K1) across, end YO, K2—183 sts.

Row 13 (WS): Purl.

YOKE

Worked over a multiple of 6 + 3 sts. See chart on page 61 for rows 14–25 if you prefer working from charts. Cont to purl WS rows.

Row 14 (RS): K1, *YO, ssk, K1, YO, K2tog, K1; rep from *, end YO, ssk.

Row 16: K2, *YO, ssk, K1, K2tog, YO, K1; rep from *, end K1.

Row 18: K3, *YO, sl 1-K2tog-psso, YO, K3; rep from *.

Row 20: K1, *YO, K2tog, K1, YO, ssk, K1; rep from *, end YO, K2tog.

Row 22: K2, *K2tog, YO, K1, YO, ssk, K1; rep from *, end K1.

Row 24: K1, K2tog, YO, *K3, YO, sl 1-K2tog-psso, YO; rep from * to last 6 sts, end last rep K3, YO, ssk, K1.

Row 25 (WS): Purl.

Row 26: K2, *YO, K1; end YO, K2—363 sts.

BODY

Rep rows 14–25 five more times or until shawl is desired length. End after working row 19 or 25.

BOTTOM EDGE

BO loosely—and you do need it to be loosely with this pattern in particular—using size 13 needle. Weave in tails and block.

Yoke and body

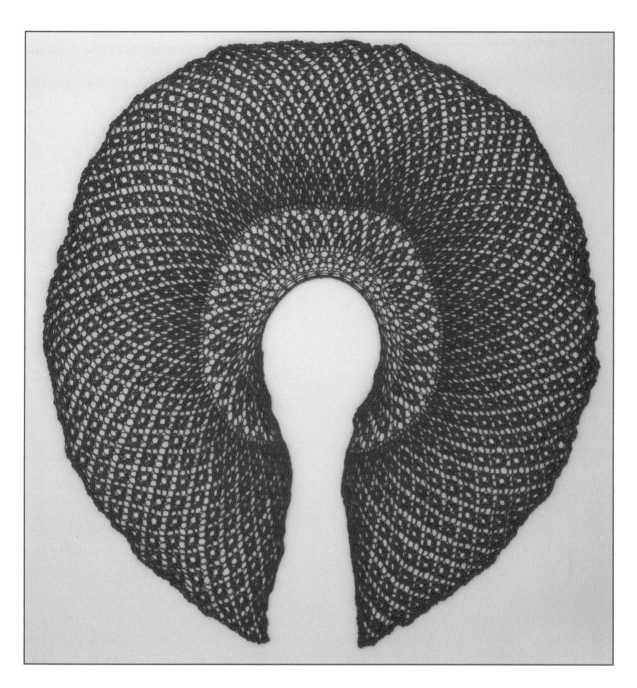

Shawl Chart
Starts on row 14 (RS).

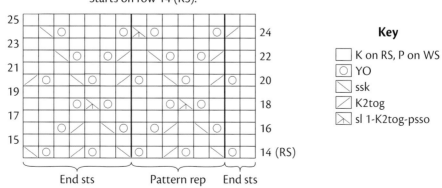

Key

☐ K on RS, P on WS

⊙ YO

◺ ssk

◿ K2tog

⧄ sl 1-K2tog-psso

Michelle's Story

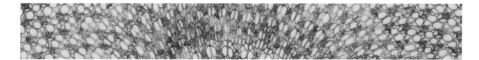

"*H*APPY MOTHER'S DAY, Mom!" Michelle said happily as I opened the package and pulled out the most gorgeous, slinky-drapey-soft yarn, which just cried out to be stroked and petted and gazed at adoringly—and knitted. Hours and hours to look forward to. My needles, this was wonderful stuff.

"Thank you!"

Sea Silk yarn is a hand-dyed blend of silk and Seacell, which is derived from kelp. I just want to know, badly, who on earth was it that first looked at a bunch of slimy green stuff washed up along the beach and thought, gee, I'd *really* like to wear that? And how long did it take them to come up with the actual spun fiber? How did they do it? Talk about a renewable resource. At the Monterey Bay Aquarium, their kelp forest grows 4" every day on the strength of sea and sun alone. I think the mermaid in Copenhagen should be wearing something like this, in the Ocean colorway.

It left me wondering what fibers our grandchildren will be knitting someday. Molted penguin pinfeathers left behind at the nesting grounds? Blown winter panda coats collected in the spring by volunteers walking the wild bamboo forests to help fund preservation efforts? Hippo nose hairs? Who knows?

I knew this shawl was already a success when my daughter said that evening, as I started working on it, "Um, Mom, I know we gave that yarn to you for Mother's Day, but just in case you need someone to give it to, I really, really like that. A lot."

I could not have asked for a better way to celebrate the day. Of course it's for her! The hope of every knitting mother: first, you get them to fall in love with the yarn. Next, maybe they'll even want to learn to cast on, too. A little purl stitch here, a yarn over there, and soon there's no stopping them. Like anything else with raising children, one patient step and stitch at a time. Onward.

Michelle's Shawl

The luster and feel of this yarn running through your hands as you knit and of the shawl on your back as you wear it is just incredible. Enjoy.

Materials

- 2 skeins of Sea Silk from Hand Maiden Fine Yarn (70% silk, 30% Seacell; 100 g; 400 m per skein) in colorway Plum
- Size 8 (5 mm) circular needle, 32" to 40" long, or size to obtain gauge
- Size 11 (8 mm) knitting needle for binding off
- Tapestry needle for weaving in tails

Skill Level

■■□□

Easy

Finished Blocked Measurements

Length: Approx 23"
Bottom Circumference: Approx 144"

Gauge

6-st rep = 2.25" over body pattern (chart B or rows 14–20), blocked

Instructions

CO 13 sts loosely, doubling yarn for the CO row and keeping sts at least 1" apart (see "Neck Edges" on page 10).

Note: For this shawl, I cast on 25 stitches and began with row 3. For a tighter neck edge, cast on 13 stitches and begin with row 1.

Row 1 (and all WS rows): Purl.

Row 2 (RS): (K1, YO) across, end K1—25 sts.

Row 4: (K1, YO) across, end K1—49 sts.

Row 6: (K1, YO) across, end K1—97 sts.

Row 7 (WS): Purl.

YOKE

Worked over a multiple of 6 + 1 sts. See chart A on page 65 for rows 8–11 if you prefer to work from charts. Cont to purl WS rows.

Row 8 (RS): K1, *YO, ssk, K1, K2tog, YO, K1; rep from *.

Row 10: K1, *YO, K1, sl 1-K2tog-psso, K1, YO, K1; rep from *.

Row 11 (WS): Purl.

Row 12: (K1, YO) across, end K1—193 sts.

BODY

Worked over a multiple of 6 + 1 sts. See chart B on page 65 for rows 14–21 if you prefer to work from charts. Cont to purl WS rows.

Row 14 (RS): Rep row 8.

Row 16: Rep row 10.

Row 18: K1, *K2tog, YO, K1, YO, ssk, K1; rep from *.

Row 20: K2tog, *(K1, YO) twice, K1, sl 1-K2tog-psso; rep from *, ending last rep with ssk instead of sl 1-K2tog-psso.

Row 21 (WS): Purl.

Row 22: *K1, YO across, end K1—385 sts.

Row 23 (WS): Purl.

Rep rows 14–21 until shawl measures approx 22" or desired length.

BOTTOM EDGE

Worked over a multiple of 12 + 1 sts. See chart C on page 65 for rows 1–10 if you prefer to work from charts.

Row 1 (RS): K1, *YO, ssk, K7, K2tog, YO, K1; rep from *.

Row 2 (and all WS rows): Purl.

Row 3: K1, *K1, YO, ssk, K5, K2tog, YO, K2; rep from *.

Row 5: K1, *(YO, ssk) twice, K3, (K2tog, YO) twice, K1; rep from *.

Row 7: K1, *K1, (YO, ssk) twice, K1, (K2tog, YO) twice, K2; rep from *.

Row 9: K1, *(YO, ssk) twice, YO, sl 1-K2tog-psso, YO, (K2tog, YO) twice, K1; rep from *.

Row 10 (WS): Purl.

BO loosely, using size 11 needle. Weave in tails and block.

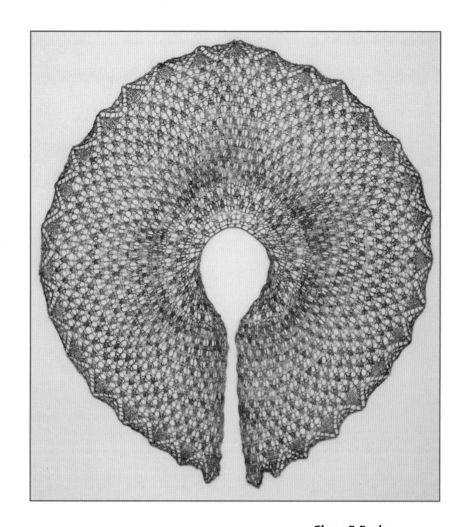

Chart A Yoke
Starts on row 8 (RS).

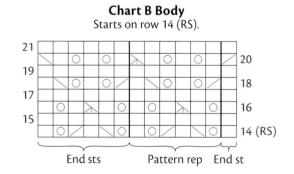

Chart B Body
Starts on row 14 (RS).

Chart C Bottom Edge
Starts on row 1 (WS).

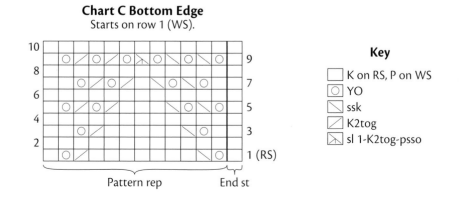

Key

☐	K on RS, P on WS
⊙	YO
◥	ssk
◢	K2tog
◩	sl 1-K2tog-psso

Karen's Story

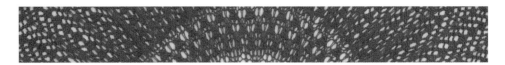

I WANTED TO SEE box turtles in the woods again while I was visiting, I told my old high-school friend. Karen and I were walking along the C&O Canal for old-times' sake. And there! A water turtle surfaced near us. A big one, ambling along. A bubble formed at its nose as it rose for air, its head came up, and then it zigged gently downwards. Zag up at an angle, then zig down yet again, never straight across the surface but taking in the water and the air in its unhurried stride.

Karen's house, when we were growing up, was set back in the woods. Every night, the raccoons would tip over the trash cans. Her chore was to clean up the mess. Finally, she thought, "Nuts to this," and she started simply leaving the cans on their sides to minimize the damage. As we watched the water turtle, she told me, remembering fondly, "The box turtles liked chicken the best." Turtles had come, too.

When Karen was 21, her mom died. Her dad remarried, and then he died, too. Helen, Karen's stepmom, was living in the house Karen had grown up in. Helen had never had children of her own, but Karen's daughter, now an adult, had had Helen as her grandma all her growing-up years. Helen was family, plain and simple. Helen was near the canal, and we decided to drop in on our way by. She greeted us warmly.

We told her about our water turtle, and she exclaimed, "Oh!" She had a turtle, too! Her home there was on a big piece of property, and at 86, living by herself, simply getting the mail or the newspaper was a bit of a trek. Karen and her family took her out for dinner once a week, but the long hours in between could get pretty lonely. But for years, a box turtle had come out of the woods right up outside her window. It had kept her company for hours, every day, right by her, making an old lady feel connected to nature, to those beautiful woods, to life itself. Then it would go back.

She didn't know why the turtle came. We didn't tell her.

Box turtles are omnivorous when they're young, vegetarians as they age. They can live a hundred years. Karen had no way of knowing, a generation ago, that she was preparing a way for her future stepmother, whom she had not then even met, to be less lonely in her old age. I knitted Helen a mohair shawl to keep her warm while going for the paper on frigid winter mornings. I knitted this one for Karen in celebration of life, of turtles, of friendship, and of love running deep through the ups and downs and zigzags of life.

Karen's Water Turtles Shawl

*This is one of the simpler shawls in this book
and uses Barbara Walker's Arrowhead Lace.*

Materials

- ◌ 7 skeins of 100% baby alpaca from Pacific Meadows Alpacas (150 yds per skein) in color Mallard **1**
- ◌ Size 9 (5.5 mm) circular needle, 32" to 40" long, or size to obtain gauge
- ◌ Size 13 (9 mm) knitting needle for binding off
- ◌ Tapestry needle for weaving in tails

Skill Level

■■□□

Easy

Finished Blocked Measurements

Length: Approx 20"
Bottom Circumference: Approx 192"

Gauge

10-st rep = 4" over body pattern (chart B or rows 38–41)

Instructions

CO 10 sts loosely, with yarn doubled for CO, keeping sts about 1" apart (see "Neck Edges" on page 10).

Row 1 (and all WS rows): Purl.

Row 2 (RS): (K1, YO) across, end K1—19 sts.

Row 4: (K1, YO) across, end K1—37 sts.

Row 6: (K1, YO) across, end K1—73 sts.

Row 8: K1, *YO, ssk, K1, K2tog, YO, K1, rep from *.

Row 10: K1, *YO, K1, sl 1-K2tog-psso, K1, YO, K1, rep from *.

Row 12: K1, (YO, K1) across—145 sts.

Row 13 (WS): Purl.

YOKE

Worked over a multiple of 6 + 1 sts. See chart A on page 69 for rows 14–21 if you prefer to work from charts. Cont to purl WS rows.

Row 14 (RS): K1, *YO, ssk, K1, K2tog, YO, K1; rep from *.

Row 16: K1, *YO, K1, sl 1-K2tog-psso, K1, YO, K1; rep from *.

Row 18: K1, *K2tog, YO, K1, YO, ssk, K1; rep from *.

Row 20: K2tog, *(K1, YO) twice, K1, sl 1-K2tog-psso; rep from *, end ssk.

Row 21 (WS): Purl.

Row 22: K1, *YO, K1; rep from *—289 sts.

Row 23: Purl.

Rows 24–35: Rep rows 14–21 once, then rep rows 14–17 once more.

Row 36 (RS): *K2, YO, K1, YO, K1, YO, K2, YO; rep from *, end K1—481 sts. This makes each group of 6 become a group of 10 that lines up correctly with it.

Row 37 (WS): Purl.

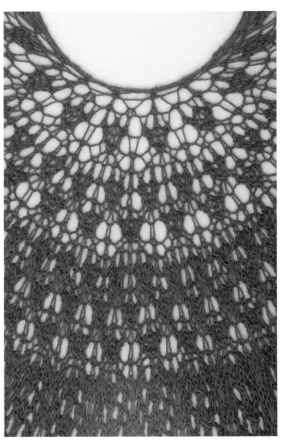

Yoke pattern

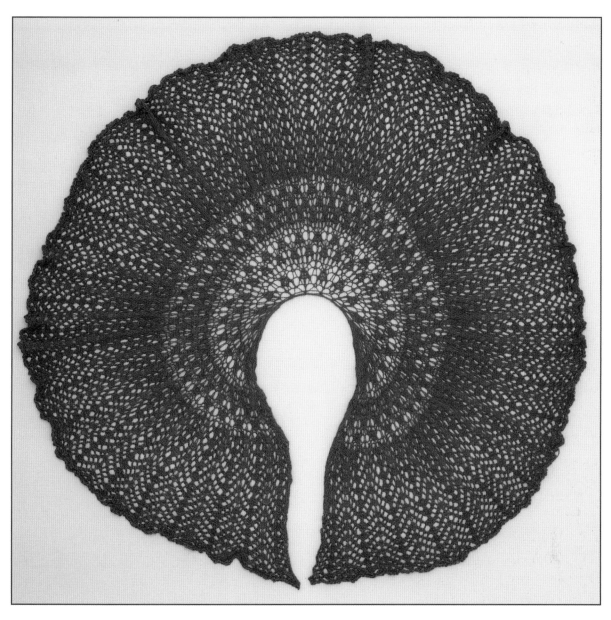

Chart A Yoke
Starts on row 14 (RS).

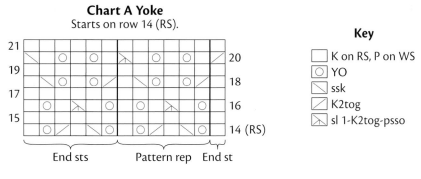

End sts   Pattern rep   End st

Key

☐ K on RS, P on WS
◯ YO
◺ ssk
◿ K2tog
⧄ sl 1-K2tog-psso

Chart B Body
Starts on row 38 (RS).

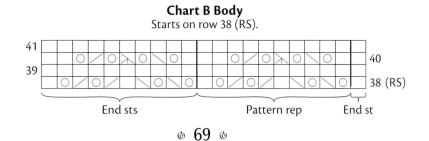

End sts   Pattern rep   End st

BODY

Worked over a multiple of 10 + 1 sts. See chart B on page 69 for rows 38–41 if you prefer to work from charts. Cont to purl WS rows.

Row 38 (RS): K1, *(YO, ssk) twice, K1, (K2tog, YO) twice, K1; rep from *.

Row 40: K2, *YO, ssk, YO, sl 2-K1-P2sso, YO, K2tog, YO, K3; rep from *, end last rep K2.

Row 41 (WS): Purl.

Rep rows 38–41 until shawl measures 20" or desired length.

BOTTOM EDGE

BO loosely, using size 13 needle. Weave in tails and block.

WATER TURTLES SHAWL (smaller version)

This 17"-long version of the Water Turtles Shawl is for those who prefer less volume. It uses 1 skein of Petal.

Needles: Size 10 and 13 circular needles, 32" to 40" long, or size to obtain gauge

Yarn: 1 skein of Petal from Lisa Souza Knitwear and Dyeworks (50% silk, 50% merino; 667 yds, ⅓ lb per skein) in color Sky Drama **①**

Gauge: 10-st rep = 4¼" over body pattern (rows 36 and 38 or chart on page 69)

With size 10 needle, CO 14 sts loosely, keeping sts an inch or slightly more apart.

Row 1 (and all WS rows): Purl.

Row 2 (RS): (YO, K1) across—28 sts.

Row 4: (K1, YO) across—55 sts.

Row 6: (K1, YO) across—109 sts.

Row 8: K1, *YO, ssk, K1, K2tog, YO, K1, rep from *.

Row 10: K1, *YO, K1, sl 1-K2tog-psso, K1, YO, K1, rep from *.

Row 12: (K1, YO) across, end K1—217 sts.

Row 13 (WS): Purl.

YOKE

Work rows 14–21 of larger shawl twice (see page 68). Continue to purl WS rows.

Row 30: Rep row 14.

Row 32: Rep row 16.

Row 34: *K2, YO, K1, YO, K1, YO, K2, YO; rep from *, end K1—361 sts. This makes each group of 6 become a group of 10 that lines up correctly with it.

Row 35 (WS): Purl.

BODY

Work as for larger shawl with rows 38–41 for patt. BO with size 13 needle.

September Story

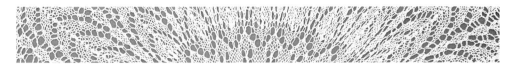

*S*ix days after September 11, 2001, I wrote the following:

We had a ceremony on the grounds of the Palo Alto City Hall last night, with leaders of the local Muslim, Jewish, Buddhist, Lutheran, Quaker, Baptist, Mormon, and Baha'i faiths represented. The audience held hands, stranger reaching out to stranger, as they spoke of hopes of peace and brotherhood and honorable living. It was very moving. (Twice, a jet passed overhead, rather unnerving standing in front of one of the tallest buildings in town.) Joan Baez, who lives in the hills above here, sang the Lord's Prayer, with the audience echoing after every line, and then her niece, Pearl Bryan, sang "Way over Yonder." It was all a strange mixture of emotion, of profound brotherhood and profound grief; at the end, the minister on the makeshift stage (an office folding table) asked for several minutes of contemplation, either silent or aloud.

With our heads bowed together, there were occasional sentences spoken into the quiet. Finally, one man proclaimed decisively, "May America always be like this." That was the perfect summing up at such a gathering of hearts.

Yet I left wondering if the whole thing was, in the end, futile. I looked at the headline in the paper this morning, "Three-Day Ultimatum," and feared it was.

But I know I felt close to all those there, no matter their background. To the young Muslim men who sang movingly from the Koran, in music different from mine and yet not, expressing their hopes that those who believed in their religion would understand it and truly live it.

And I hope I remember, despite my stress and my fear for my nearly draft-age son, to live mine as well, moment by moment, in kindness and brotherly love toward every soul created by God.

I'm sure there were moments like that shared all across the country in the times shortly following that unendurable day, when my own brother was one of the lucky ones who called home and said, "Mom. Dad. My subway was late. I'm OK." I was so afraid as I left those grounds that what was resonating so deeply in my soul would have no meaning in the overall context of the world. And yet, to me, it resonates still. Enough that my knitter's soul needed to put it into stitches and my writer's soul needed to make the words more permanent. Thus I have created this shawl, in white to radiate light to remind me never to treat anyone with shortness of thought or heart. The pattern, to my eyes, shows anchors around the shoulders to remind us who we most deeply are. Below, hands reach out to hold the hands of others. Standing together in our humanity.

Peace of My Mind Shawl

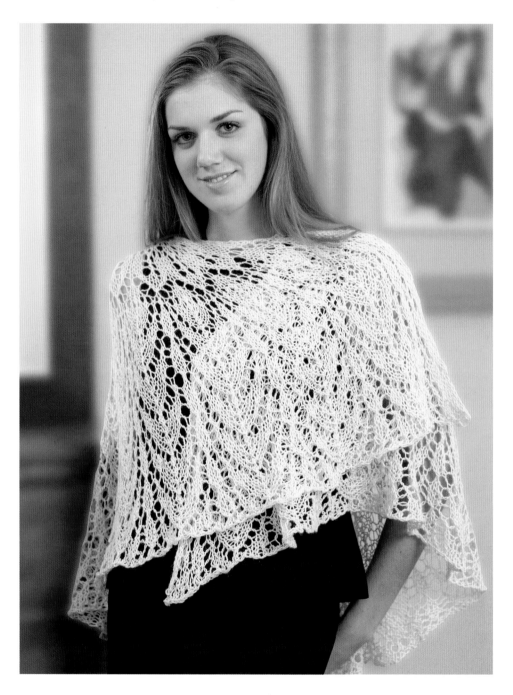

Barbara Walker's Fountain Lace, knitted from the top down, looks like paper cutout figures of people holding hands. The silk gives it the subtle radiance I had hoped for when I chose this yarn.

Materials

- ❧ 10 skeins of Baby Silk from Peruvian Collection (80% baby alpaca, 20% silk; 25 g; 109 yds per skein) in color 100 ❶
- ❧ Size 9 (5.5 mm) circular needle, 32" to 40" long, or size to obtain gauge
- ❧ Size 13 (9 mm) knitting needle for binding off
- ❧ Tapestry needle for weaving in tails

Skill Level

◼◼◼☐
Intermediate

Finished Blocked Measurements

Length: Approx 20"
Bottom Circumference: Approx 144"

Gauge

16-st rep = 6" over body pattern (chart B or rows 30–37), blocked

Instructions

CO 12 sts loosely, doubling yarn for the CO row and keeping sts at least 1" apart (see "Neck Edges" on page 10).

Row 1 (and all WS rows): Purl.

Row 2: (YO, K1) across—24 sts.

Row 4: (YO, K1) across—48 sts.

Row 6: (YO, K1) across—96 sts.

Row 8: K2, *K2tog, YO, K1; rep from *, end K1.

Row 10: K2, *YO, K1, K2tog; rep from *, end K1.

Row 12: Rep row 8.

Row 14: (YO, K1) across to last st, YO, lift bar below next st and knit into that, knit last st—193 sts.

Row 15 (WS): Purl.

YOKE

Worked over a multiple of 8 + 1 sts. See chart A on page 74 for rows 16–27 if you prefer working from charts. Cont to purl WS rows.

Rows 16, 18, and 20 (RS): K1, *K2, YO, sl 1-K2tog-psso, YO, K3; rep from *.

Row 22: K1, *YO, ssk, K3, K2tog, YO, K1; rep from *.

Row 24: K1, *K1, YO, ssk, K1, K2tog, YO, K2; rep from *.

Row 26: K1, *K2, YO, sl 1-K2tog-psso, YO, K3; rep from *.

Row 27 (WS): Purl.

Row 28: K1, YO across, end K1—385 sts.

Row 29: Purl.

BODY

Worked over a multiple of 16 + 1 sts. See chart B on page 74 for rows 30–37 if you prefer working from charts. Cont to purl WS rows.

Row 30 (RS): Ssk, *YO, K2, K2tog, YO, K1, YO, sl 1-K2tog-psso, YO, K1, YO, ssk, K2, YO, sl 1-K2tog-psso; rep from *, end last rep K2tog.

Row 32: Ssk, *K3, YO, K2tog, YO, K3, YO, ssk, YO, K3, sl 1-K2tog-psso; rep from *, end last rep K2tog.

Row 34: Ssk, *(K2, YO) twice, K2tog, K1, ssk, (YO, K2) twice, sl 1-K2tog-psso; rep from *, end last rep K2tog.

Row 36: Ssk, *K1, YO, K3, YO, K2tog, K1, ssk, YO, K3, YO, K1, sl 1-K2tog-psso; rep from *, end last rep K2tog.

Row 37 (WS): Purl.

Rep rows 30–37 five more times or until shawl is desired length.

BOTTOM EDGE

Next row (RS): Rep row 30.

Next row (WS): Purl.

BO loosely, using size 13 needle. Weave in tails and block.

Chart A Yoke
Starts on row 16 (RS).

Pattern rep | End st

Key

☐ K on RS, P on WS
⊡ YO
◻ ssk
◻ K2tog
⋈ sl 1-K2tog-psso

Chart B Body
Starts on row 30 (RS).

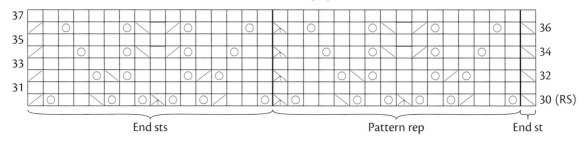

End sts | Pattern rep | End st

Barn Swallows Story

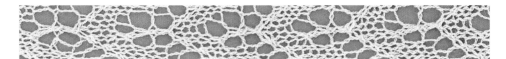

$\mathcal{M}$Y SON JOHN was given an extra-credit assignment by his history teacher to go watch a Civil War reenactment coming up on the weekend. Civil War reenactors? In California? Growing up in Maryland, I'd known people who were really into that, but I'd thought it was very much a southeastern-U.S. thing—history buffs trying to get close to their ancestors. I was assured by the teacher, "Oh, no, it's a big thing here, too. Go see."

So I packed up the kid and we went. John and I listened to a die-hard confederate in graying beard and uniform, a man who spent his time traveling from reenactment to reenactment, telling the history of his officer and of the engagement at hand in great detail. I later chatted with a woman at a spinning wheel, trying not to break character for her but recognizing the modern model and make of her wheel. I told her, my grandmother's grandmother, born in 1814, was considered very old-fashioned because she still spun. She took her wheel across the plains in her covered wagon, sure it would be forever before she could buy store-bought again; but I think that was partly to justify its weight to the wagon master. I think she wanted the comfort of the rhythm of the wheel to sustain her in times and in strange places she could not quite see yet, but were soon to come down the road, to help make unfamiliar country begin to be home.

We sat down on the side of the field and watched the battle beginning to take place, the Blue versus the Gray, the cavalry versus the foot soldiers. Horses charged, cannons fired. You certainly couldn't talk over it all. You could only bear witness to what man once had done to man, brother to brother, right here in our own land.

There was a pavilion there at the Felton fairgrounds, and a number of barn swallows were flitting in and out, taking care of their young in the nests hanging from the rafters. With the crowds milling around and the booms going off nearby, the swallows reacted to it all with a southern accent, as in, they didn't pay it no never-mind. They had work to do—living, taking care of the things that mattered to them, not letting the unusual to-do get in the way. Holding to the rhythms that sustain them, flitting from nest to food to nest.

Barn swallows, flying home. This is my version of them from the twigs and fibers I create with here in my hands, a place of peace coming to be as I knit.

Barn Swallows Scarf

I gave this scarf to Ann Rubin to thank her for her work with afghans for Afghans, which provides warm, handknit woolen items to people in need in Afghanistan, and lets knitters reach out to their fellow beings, peacemaking, one to one.

Materials

- ⚘ 1 skein of Zephyr Silk/Wool from JaggerSpun (50% Chinese tussah silk, 50% fine merino wool; 2 oz; 630 yds per skein) in color Mushroom
- ⚘ Size 7 (4.5 mm) needles or size to obtain gauge
- ⚘ Tapestry needle for weaving in tails

Skill Level

Intermediate

Finished Blocked Measurements

Length: Approx 56"
Width: Approx 4"

Gauge

21-st rep = 4½" over body pattern (chart or rows 6–15), blocked

Instructions

CO 21 sts.

See chart below for all rows if you prefer to work from charts.

TOP BORDER

Row 1 (and all WS rows): Purl.

Row 2 (RS): K1, (YO, K2tog) across.

Row 4: K1, YO, K2tog, knit to last 3 sts, ssk, YO, K1.

SCARF BODY

Row 6: K1, YO, K2tog, K2, YO, ssk, K2, YO, sl 1-K2tog-psso, YO, K2, K2tog, YO, K2, ssk, YO, K1.

Row 8: K1, YO, K2tog, K3, YO, ssk, K2, YO, K2tog, K1, K2tog, YO, K3, ssk, YO, K1.

Row 10: K1, YO, K2tog, K4, YO, ssk, K3, K2tog, YO, K4, ssk, YO, K1.

Row 12: K1, YO, K2tog, K5, YO, ssk, K1, K2tog, YO, K5, ssk, YO, K1.

Row 14: K1, YO, K2tog, K6, YO, sl 1-K2tog-psso, YO, K6, ssk, YO, K1.

Row 15 (WS): Purl.

Rep rows 6–15 until scarf measures 55" or 1" less than desired length.

BOTTOM BORDER

See rows 16–19 of chart if you prefer to work from charts.

Next RS row: Rep row 4.

Next RS row: Rep row 2.

Next row (WS): Purl.

BO all sts.

Scarf Chart
Starts on row 1 (WS).

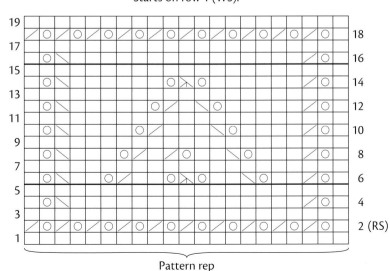

Pattern rep

Key

- ☐ K on RS, P on WS
- ⊡ YO
- ⟍ ssk
- ⟋ K2tog
- ⟑ sl 1-K2tog-psso

Abbreviations and Conversions

Terms and Abbreviations

approx	approximately
beg	beginning
BO	bind off
CO	cast on
cont	continue
dec	decrease
frog	to take the stitches off the needles and rip out the knitting, an Internet term that is a pun on the *rip-it, rip-it, rip-it* sound that a frog makes
g	gram
inc	increase
K	knit
K2tog	knit 2 stitches together as 1 (decrease)
K3tog	knit 3 stitches together as 1 (double decrease)
lb	pound
M1	make 1 stitch: lift horizontal strand between the needles from front to back and place on left-hand needle; knit through back loop of stitch formed
oz	ounces
P	purl
P2tog	purl 2 stitches together as 1 (decrease)
P2tog-tbl	purl 2 stitches together through the back loop
P3tog	purl 3 stitches together as 1 (double decrease)
P3tog-tbl	purl 3 stitches together through the back loop (double decrease)
psso	pass slipped stitch(es) over
rem	remaining
rep	repeat
RS	right side
sl	slip
sl 1-K2tog-psso	slip 1, knit 2 together, pass the slipped stitch over
sl 2-K1-p2sso	slip 2 stitches together as if to knit, knit 1, pass the 2 slipped stitches over
ssk	slip, slip, knit
st(s)	stitch(es)
tog	together
WS	wrong side
yds	yards
YO	yarn over

Metric Conversions

m	=	yds	x	0.9144
yds	=	m	x	1.0936
g	=	oz	x	28.35
oz	=	g	x	0.0352

Charitable Organizations

afghans for Afghans
www.afghansforafghans.org

Books

A Treasury of Knitting Patterns and *A Second Treasury of Knitting Patterns* by Barbara Walker. Schoolhouse Press, 1998. Worth many times their weight in qiviut.

Dyes

Dharma Trading Company
PO Box 150916
San Rafael, CA 94915
(800) 542-5227
www.dharmatrading.com

Music

Bing Concert Series, Stanford Hospital, Stanford, CA, 94305
Joan Baez, www.joanbaez.com
KFJC 89.7 FM, kfjc.org, Foothill College's radio station in Los Altos Hills, CA
Karen Bentley Pollick, www.kbentley.com

Yarns

Blue Sky Alpacas, Inc.
PO Box 88
Cedar, MN 55011
(888) 460-8862
www.blueskyalpacas.com
Wholesale only

Fleece Artist Hand Maiden Yarns
1174 Mineville Rd.
Mineville, Nova Scotia B2Z 1K8
Canada
www.fleeceartist.com
Wholesale only

Frog Tree Yarns
T and C Imports
PO Box 1119
East Dennis, MA 02641
(508) 385-8862
www.frogtreeyarns.com

JaggerSpun
Water St.
Springvale, ME 04083
www.jaggeryarn.com
Wholesale only

Knitpicks
13118 NE 4th St.
Vancouver, WA 98684
(360) 260-8900
www.knitpicks.com

Kpixie Yarns
(508) 378-7344
www.kpixie.com
My retail source for Blue Sky Alpacas yarn

Lisa Souza Knitwear and Dyeworks
(925) 283-4058
www.lisaknit.com
All kinds of hand-dyed yarns

Pacific Meadows Alpacas
PO Box 634
Junction City, OR 97448
(541) 579-8352
www.alpacanation.com/pacificmeadows.asp
Fingering-weight baby alpaca in hanks or cones

Rowan
Green Lane Mill
Holmfirth
HD9 2DX England
www.knitrowan.com

Tess' Designer Yarns
33 Strawberry Point
Steuben, ME 04680
(800) 321-TESS
www.tessyarns.com

wiseNeedle
www.wiseneedle.com
Independently run Web site with general knitting advice and much information on individual yarns as critiqued by the general public

Lace Blocking Wires

Halcyon Yarn
12 School St.
Bath, ME 04530
(800) 341-0282
www.halcyonyarn.com

HandWorks Northwest, LLC
PO Box 19322
Portland, OR 97219
lisa@handworksnw.com
www.handworksnw.com
A portion of the proceeds is donated to the Susan G. Komen Breast Cancer Foundation

Knitpicks
13118 NE 4th St.
Vancouver, WA 98684
(360) 260-8900
www.knitpicks.com

About the Author

ALISON JEPPSON HYDE was born in Washington, DC, and grew up in Bethesda, Maryland, the fourth of six children of an art dealer and author father and a musically gifted schoolteacher mother. Her folks built a house with tall picture windows in the woods alongside Cabin John Regional Park, where she and her siblings hiked the trails built by the Civilian Conservation Corps in the 1930s. The C&O Canal National Park and the Potomac River were nearby.

Sixteen years of systemic lupus and Crohn's, which began when her youngest was two, have taught her to appreciate the gift that those years gave her: the imperative need to create something beautiful and an ample amount of time at home in which to do so. Knitting became her passion, a way to take time and love and make them tangible—a way to make a difference. Giving a wedding ring shawl to one of her doctors for his wife, a woman she had never met, when she was new at lace knitting, taught her to give fearlessly of herself, and that knitting could convey a message of great gratitude to a degree that words perhaps could not. She learned to appreciate how a few ounces of good yarn can help her befriend the people around her. She is infinitely grateful for an artistic mother who taught her to knit.

Alison and her husband, Richard, live in Palo Alto, California, and are the parents of two sons and two daughters.

ACKNOWLEDGMENTS

First of all, I want to thank my sweet husband, Richard Hyde, for putting the idea in my head to create this book and then seeing me through the process. I also want to thank my children, Jennie, Richard, Michelle, and John, and my son-in-law, Jonathan Pratt-Ferguson, for cheering me on.

A thank-you to my friend and neighbor Gracie Larsen of the Lacy Knitters Guild and founder of the Lace Museum in Sunnyvale, California, for her encouraging words. A thank-you to Barbara Walker for her generosity in allowing me to use her lace stitch patterns extensively throughout the book. Warm hugs to my test knitters Susan Clueitz, Eve Brasfield, Gigi Karimzadeh, Constance Harker, Lisa Keating, and Pam Jajko for your help; I couldn't have done this book without your needles, your friendship, and your time confirming my stitches with your own.

And to my other friends mentioned in these pages: Kathy; Dave; Wanda; Nina and Rod Price; Virginia and Daniel Hosford; Michelle Romero; Lisa, Michael, David, Jonathan, Tara, and William Jibson; Karen Lewis; Lisa Souza; Julia, Brandon, and Camille Jacobsen; Constance Harker; and Henry. Thanks to Terry Martin, formerly of Martingale, for her enthusiasm. Thanks to Donna Druchunas for all her technical help, and Tina Cook and Mary Green for their editing.

And a heartfelt thanks to Dr. Paul Rubinstein, who willed me to live and pulled me through a critical illness in July '03, thus granting me the time on this planet that nearly every stitch and word in this book was created in. Thank you for being there for me and for helping me want to give back to everybody with what you gave me then. My life. —Alison Hyde